КУЇВ

D1724366

1. Rosenberg's Synagogue
2. Naberezhno-Mykilska Church
3. Samson fountaine
4. St. Flor's Convent
5. Holy Intercession Monastery
6. Circus
7. Railway station
8. St. Volodymyr's Cathedral
9. The Golden gates
10. St. Sophia Cathedral
11. St. Andrew's Church
12. St. Michael's
    Golden-Domed Cathedral
13. The Column of Magdeburg Law
14. The Arch of Peoples' Friendship
15. St. Alexander's Roman
    Catholic Cathedral
16. The Column of Independence
17. The house of Taras Shevchenko
18. The Lesya Ukrainka Russian
    Drama Theater
19. The Taras Shevchenko National
    Museum
20. The National Opera of Ukraine
21. Bohdan and Varvara Khanenko
    Museum of Art and
    the Museum of Russian Art
22. The monument to Taras
    Shevchenko
23. St. Nicolas' Roman
    Catholic Cathedral
24. Olimpiysky National
    Sports Complex
25. The Kosyi Kaponir
    fortress-museum
26. Choral Synagogue
27. The House with Chimeras
28. The International Center of
    Culture and Arts
29. The National Art Museum of
    Ukraine
30. The Verkhovna Rada of Ukraine
31. Mariinsky Palace
32. Pedestrian Bridge
33. Metro Bridge
34. The Eternal Glory monument
35. Kyiv Pechersk Lavra
36. The National Museum of
    the History of the Great
    Patriotic War
37. Vydubytsky Monastery

Дніпро
Dnipro

Лаврська
Lavrska

Ігнатенська

Moskovska

Кутузова
Kutuzova

Lesi Ukrainky

Печерська
Pecherska

Дружби Народів
Druzhby Narodiv

Дружби Народів
Druzhby Narodiv

Палац Україна
Palats Ukraina

Chervonoarmiyska (V. Vasylkivska)

Антоновича
Antonovycha

Либідська
Lybidska

«THE CITIES OF UKRAINE»

УДК 908 (477-25) (084.12)=161

"THE CITIES OF UKRAINE" series

Front cover:
In the centre – Maidan Nezalezhnosti (Independence Square),
The Puppet Theatre,
The monument to the founders of Kyiv,
T. Shevchenko National Opera,
Vydubytsky monastery in the spring,
The Golden gates,
The Verkhovna Rada (Parliament) of Ukraine,
Monument to Bohdan Khmelnytsky,
The main building of T. Shevchenko National University,
St. Volodymyr's Cathedral,
The Cabinet of Ministers of Ukraine,
The 'Motherland' monument,
St. Michael's Cathedral,
St. Nicholas' Roman Catholic Cathedal,
'Samson' fountain,
Mariinsky Palace,
Vydubytsky monastery in the autumn,
The House with Chimeras,
The composition from the flower exhibition in Pechersk Landscape Park.
First page – Kyiv Pechersk Lavra. Cupola of the Bell Tower at the Far Caves
Back cover – Moskovsky (Moscow) Bridge

ISBN 978-966-543-086-7 (series)   Copyright © 2004, 2005, 2006, 2009, 2010, 2011, 2013, 2016
                                   by Vakler Publishing Company, Ltd.
ISBN 978-966-543-106-0   Copyright © Text by Sergei Udovik, 2004, 2005, 2006, 2009, 2010,
                                   2011, 2013, 2016

Sergei Udovik

K Y I V

Photo book
The eighth edition, revised and supplemented

Kyiv
Vakler Publishing Company

Kyiv occupies a special place among cities of the world. It is not only the largest political, economic and cultural centre of Eastern Europe – not many cities of the world had the honour to become the cradle of one of the world's civilizations, Slavonic-Orthodox – but Kyiv has also one more merit: irreplaceable charm, created by a unique combination of picturesque hills; endless Dnieper expanses; and golden-domed churches nestled among verdant fields. Kyiv is located on the boundary of vast endless forests beginning in France and steppes stretching to China. Forest and steppe, high right bank and low left bank, the West and the East meet in Kyiv and combine in harmony facilitated by the great Dnieper. The river divides and unites the city creating a number of channels within Kyiv and forming landscapes of staggering beauty, which can be observed enchantingly for hours from high right bank.

Kyiv is also considered to be a spiritual-mystical city. It is open to the sun, the sky, and water and possesses strong positive energy. Apparently this environment promoted the shaping of a philosophical world-view among Kyivites. The location of Kyiv between East and West created a multicultural atmosphere of tolerance, benevolence and hospitality. In Kyiv, many Orthodox churches coexist peacefully with churches of other Christian denominations: Catholic, Greek Catholic, Protestant, as well as synagogues, mosques and other houses of worship. In Kyiv you can also see the most ancient Orthodox monasteries. The most famous among them is Kyiv-Pechersk Lavra.

At the same time Kyiv is a very modern city, which closely grasps the trends of world development. It is here that a strong scientific potential is concentrated. Modern communications connect Kyiv with all corners of the world.

One of the unique features of Kyiv is that in a city of three million people you can easily seclude yourself within nature – either in one of the numerous parks or gardens which are spread throughout the city, or near lakes, or in forest parks surrounding Kyiv. Thus Kyiv is called a garden city, a city where it is possible to combine business life with relaxation easily. It is especially magnificent in spring, in May, when lilacs bloom, when magnolias exude their fragrance under the open sky, and beautiful chestnuts spread open their flower-candle blossoms. Those who visit Kyiv in May retain an indelible sensation of contact with the divine for the rest of their lives, because only God could create such miraculous beauty.

Spring in Lavra

At the Dnieper

The History of Kyiv

The history of Kyiv began in ancient days. The first human settlements appeared on the territory of present-day Kyiv at the end of the Stone Age, about 20 thousand years ago. One of these sites, Kyrylivska, named after one of Kyiv's streets, contained the bones of 67 specimens of mammoths. Models of ancient dwellings are exhibited in the **National Natural Science Museum** (http://museumkiev.org).

There are excavated settlements of highly developed Trypillya culture dating back three thousand years B.C. on the territory of Kyiv. Contemporary to Sumerian civilization, it still keeps many mysteries, especially concerning its origin and disappearance.

According to the legend, Kyiv was founded by three brothers: *Kyi, Schek,* and *Khoryv,* and their sister *Lybid*. The town was named after the eldest brother, Kyi. Schekavytsya hill in Kyiv was named after the second brother, Schek, and the other hill, Khorevytsya, was named after the third brother, Khoryv. The river Lybid in Kyiv was named in honour of their sister. There are several monuments dedicated to the legendary founders of Kyiv.

Historians ascribe the founding of the city to the time around 5th-6th cc. An uninterrupted history of the city can be traced from that period on. By the end of the 10th c. the city became the capital of the powerful state, Kyivan Rus, and an influential political centre of Europe. The wealth and influence of Kyiv were due to trade. The city was located on the crossroads of international trading routes, the legendary one 'from the Varangians to the Greeks', i.e. from the Baltic Sea to Constantinople, and the second major route, from Regensburg through Prague, Kyiv, and further on to Asia Minor and Persia. Kyiv was also actively engaged in commerce with England.

The numerous family relations of Kyiv princes with the reigning houses of Europe are evidence of the influence and importance of Kyiv. Princess Anna, sister of Byzantine emperors, refused Emperor Otto II in favour of Prince *Volodymyr* (980-1015), the Baptiser of Rus. Kyiv Prince *Yaroslav the Wise* (1019-1054) was married to the daughter of the Swedish king, and his son Vsevolod I, to the daughter of the Byzantine Emperor Constantine Monomakh. The daughter of Yaroslav the Wise, *Elisabeth*, married Norwegian Prince *Harald*, who composed songs in her honour. Scandinavian sagas

The view on Pechersk, the Dnieper and the left bank
Rainbow over the Dnieper

On pages 8-9:
The view on Vydubytsky monastery (11th-19th cc.) from M. Hryshko Botanical Gardens

The diorama of ancient Kyiv of the 10th-13th cc. in the National Museum of the History of Ukraine

The framework of dwelling of mammoth bones (Upper Paleolithic). The National Natural Science Museum

poetically extol how the young man in love flew in his thoughts to the 'Russian beauty' and tried to win her hand. *Anastasiya* married *Andrew of Hungary*, and *Anna*, the French King *Henry I*. After his death *Anna* governed France as regent and came to be known in French history as Anne de Russie, Reine de France. Prince *Volodymyr Monomakh* (1113-1125) was married to the daughter of the English king.

In 11th c. in Kyiv there were 400 churches, 8 markets and 50,000 inhabitants, that is more than in London or Hamburg, which both had the population of 20,000 only. Among the cities of Western Europe, only Paris with population of 100,000 was bigger than Kyiv. Kyiv set an extremely high level of culture, which was followed by other cities of Rus. Here chronicles were written, magnificent temples (St. Sophia Cathedral), schools of icon-painting and splendid jewelry techniques (filigree, niello, enamel, granulation) appeared. *Batu* Khan, having seen Kyiv from the hill now called Batyeva (Batu) hill, he was struck with the greatness and beauty of the city. For 10 weeks inhabitants of Kyiv heroically battled the countless troops of *Batu*. **The Golden gates** turned out a hard nut for invaders to crack. The Mongol-Tatars managed to break through the powerful fortifications of Kyiv only at a side of Pechersk gate located in the northern part of the present-day area of **Independence Square**, which at that time was covered with forests and marshes. But even then Kyivites did not surrender, but continued to protect their beloved city up to the last citadel, the strong stone Desyatynna Church of the Mother of God, which had been constructed in the year 998. However, the Mongol-Tatars succeeded in destroying its walls with catapults. The cathedral collapsed, and under its ruins a multitude of people was buried. Untill these days **the foundation of Desyatynna Church** reminds us of these events. And by the ruins of the temple the yearly blossoming of the majestic **linden tree** for more than 400 years reminds us of the heroism of the people of Kyiv. The invasion of the Mongol-Tatars in the year 1240 brought about an irreparable loss of power to Kyiv. Enraged at the up to then unprecedented resistance by the defenders of Kyiv, the Mongol-Tatars ruthlessly plundered and destroyed the city. Thereafter life in Kyiv slowed down for a long time, and the Upper Town was left to lie in ruins. Having protected Europe from Mongol-Tatars, Kyivan Rus became dependent on the Horde for many years.

St. Nicholas' Church (1810) at Askoldova Mohyla (Askold's Grave). In 882 Varangian prince Oleg killed Kyiv princes Askold and Dir at this place

The monument to the founders of Kyiv (2000, by A. Kusch) – Kyi, Schek, Khoryv, and their sister Lybid

Life in Kyiv began to recover only in the second half of the 14th c. after entering into the structure of the Great Duchy of Lithuania and Rus (GDL). At the close of the 14th c. Prince *Volodymyr Olgerdovych* erected a fortress and a castle on the 80-meter-high steep hill. That is why the hill had gained the name of Zamkova (i.e. Castle). The fortress had massive earthworks and wooden fortifications along all the perimeter of the hill. It became the residence of Kyiv princes for many years. Crimean khans, particularly *Edigu* in 1416, tried to seize the fortress many times, but without much success. And only in 1482, *Menli Giray* managed to do this. He burned down the fortress and the castle. In the early 16th c. the fortress was restored. The fortified wall was strengthened with 15 three-storeyed towers with canons. The fortress had two entrances – Drabsky (Tramp) gates (for soldiers) with lift bridge and Voyevodsky (General's) gates. On the horologium, which faced Podil, there was a chiming clock. On the fortress' territory (with an area of 1.6 hectares) there was a palace, three Orthodox and one Roman church, houses of nobility. A garrison was also located here. In 1651 the castle was burned down by Cossacks. It had not been restored, because the construction of a new fortress in Pechersk began (see **Kyiv Fortresses**).

11

The Golden Gate in Kyiv (1862, Napoleon Orda)

The National Museum of the History of Ukraine with the remains of the foundation of Desyatynna Church (10th c.)

For three centuries, Kyiv carried out the important strategic role of protecting the territories of the GDL, and after 1569 of the Polish Lithuanian Commonwealth as well, from cruel and ruthless attacks of the Golden Horde and the Crimean Khanate armies. Kyiv was called the 'gateway to the entire Lithuanian state'. In 1422 Polish King *Vladislav II (Jagiello)* married the daughter of Kyiv Prince *Andrew Olshansky* 17-year old Princess *Sonya (Sofia, 1405-1461)*. Their third son *Kazimir Yagelonchik*, King of Poland, initiated dynasty of the *Jagiellonians*. Under Prince *Simeone Olelkovich* borders of the Kyiv Apanage Principality covered vast areas from the river Pripyat to the Black Sea. *Simeone Olelkovich* used to be called "The Kyiv Tsar". In 1740 he restored the Dormition Cathedral at Lavra and covered its domes with gold, and interiors – with rich painting. The Dormition Cathedral was a burial vault for many princes and representatives of noble families. There were mother of a Great Prince of Lithuania Jagiello, rusinka, Tver Princess *Uliana* (†1392) and Hetman GDL Prince. *K.-I. Ostrozhsky* (†1533) among them. Kiev became a large trading center, controled the Dnipro path and trade routes from Europe to Moscow Rus.

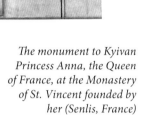

In 1596 the union with Rome was concluded in Brest. Most of Orthodox hierarchs, headed by Prince. K.-V. Ostrozhsky, opposed the union. The center of struggle against uniatism and polish gentry moved from Lviv to Kyiv. The intelligent forces of Rus concentrated here. St. Sophia Cloister, headed by Metropolitan *P. Mogila*, and Kiev-Pecherskaya Laura became a centre of opposition. The Cossacks acted as defenders of rusins' interests. In 1648 the Liberation war of rusin-ukrainians against Polish rule, in which Kyiv acted the important part, began, headed by *B. Khmelnitsky*.

In the 17th c., being protected by Cossacks, Kyiv began to rebuild and restore its numerous churches and monasteries actively. Hetman *Ivan Mazepa* was especially prominent in the field of church building. With his own funds he restored **Kyiv-Pechersk Lavra** and surrounded it with a six-meter-high strong stone wall. It also served as a fortress wall, thus the monastery transformed into a citadel. With the assistance of Hetman Mazepa **Holy gates** and **Farming gates** were built with **All Saints' Church** (1696-1698) above the latter; you can see the hetman's family **coat of arms** on its façade. With the hetman's efforts a very beautiful and grand Church of St. Nicholas was built in St. Nikolas' Hermitage Monastery. Unfortunately, it was completely destroyed during the time of Stalin. **Mazepa's house** still stands in Kyiv, and the **Museum of Ukrainian Hetmans** is now located there.

In the middle of the 18th c. majestic buildings of **St. Sophia Bell Tower** (1740ˢ) and **Great Lavra Belfry** (1731-1745); the complex of buildings at **St. Flor's Convent**; **Intercession Church** (1766); the **Hostyny Dvir** (smth like shopping arcades) in Podil; and many others were built.

In the second half of the 18th c., after Russian troops had defeated the Ottoman Empire, southern Ukrainian lands were incorporated into Ukraine. Kyiv became the centre of the Southwestern Territory of the Russian Empire, and a new period of city's development began.

In 1797 the Magdeburg law was reestablished in Kyiv. It is the right of self-government, which the city had possessed since the end of the 15th c. In honour of this event, the **Column of the Magdeburg Law** was erected in 1802 in Kyiv near the Dnieper at the place where Prince Volodymyr baptised his sons.

International trade was booming, and in 1815-1817 the **Contract House** was built as the centre of Kyiv's trade fairs. It still graces Podil. Brokers and notaries gathered there. On the second floor there was a concert hall, where *Angelica Catalani* sang and *Franz Liszt* perf ormed. *T. Shevchenko, A. Pushkin, N. Gogol, A. Mickiewicz,* and *H. de Balzac* had visited this concert hall. The latter called Kyiv the eternal city of the North, Northern Rome. He said: 'Even if I had no friends living near Kyiv, I would still travel to Kyiv because of my interest in literature and ethnography.'

Kontraktova Square would fill up with small shops on fair days. Many people would crowd into Kyiv to visit these fairs. Prices for hotel rooms would increase dramatically, therefore those who were poorer would sleep in the open air around **the fountain** called '**Samson**' (1749), which was

The monument to Kyivan Princess Anna, the Queen of France, at the Monastery of St. Vincent founded by her (Senlis, France)

The Church of the Dormition of the Mother of God (Pyrohoscha)

The monument to the Princess Olha, Sts. Cyril and Methodius Equal to the Apostles, and the Holy Apostle Andrew the First-Called (1911, 1996, sc. I. Kavaleridze)

the part of the first Kyiv's water supply. The water came here from the springs of Starokyivska hill. There was a legend connected with this fountain which said that a person who drank water from 'Samson' would stay in Kyiv forever. In the 1930ˢ the fountain was demolished upon the pretext that it was a source for spreading infections, since a tremendous amount of people wanted to drink from it. Fortunately, it was rebuilt in 1982 in its original form, but the original wood carved statue of Samson is kept in the **National Art Museum of Ukraine** now.

In 1834 the University of St. Prince Vladimir (now the University of T. Shevchenko) was opened in Kyiv. In 1830-1840-ies a huge **main building** ("red") and **Botanic Garden** was laid out for it, an **astronomical observatory** (supervised by outstanding astronomer *V. Struve*), **dissecting room** were built. The Imperial Archeographic Committee was created to study of early texts at the University. *Taras Shevchenko* worked there as a painter in 1845-1846. In 1838-1842 stately building of Institute for Noble Maidens was built in the late classical style (by *V. Beretti*). Located on a hill, the building and an adjacent park look perfectly well as viewed from Khreschatyk. Young ladies

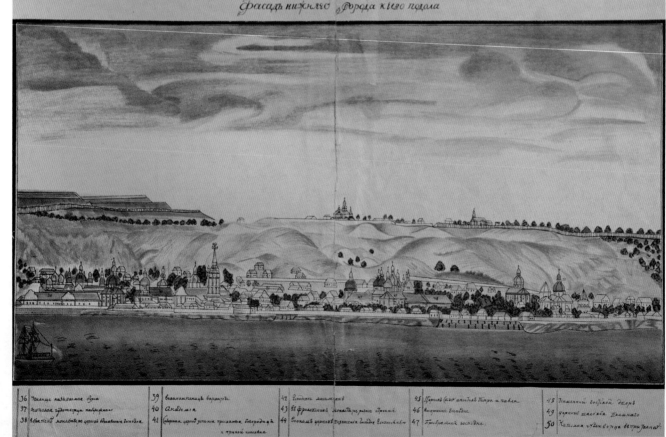

from noble and merchant families were given an excellent education here. In the 1950s the building was reconstructed into the Palace of Culture with a concert hall for 2000 seats (now – **The International Centre of Culture and Arts**).

At the beginning of the 19th c. Kyiv essentially consisted of three independent sectors Podil, Pechersk, and the Upper Town. Each of them had its own administration. The Upper Town was administered by St. Sophia's and St. Michael's Monasteries. Pechersk was governed by the general-governor and partly by Kyiv-Pechersk Lavra. Podil was ruled by the magistrate using the right of self-government. In the 1830s Aleksandrovskaya Street (present-day Hrushevskoho Street, Volodymyrsky Descent and Sahaidachnoho Street) and Bibikovsky Boulevard (now Shevchenko Boulevard) were built, uniting these three sectors of the city into one.

After this, a lot of new buildings were constructed on Khreschatyk, and in the 1870s the administrative centre of Kyiv was moved there.

Kyiv had transformed into the biggest transport junction in Eastern Europe and became the 'Sugar Capital' of Europe. In 1905 the State Bank office building was opened. Nowadays the National Bank of Ukraine is located there. The building that was added in 1934 stands out for its exquisite elements of early renaissance architecture. It is guarded by 30 lion figures. The coats of arms of Kyiv, Podilla, and Volhyn provinces are displayed on both sides of the portal entrance. Inside the bank there is a museum, which houses a rich collection of precious gems and valuables as well as different kinds of money that passed in Ukraine.

At the end of the 19th c. and at the beginning of the 20th c. the city was developing very rapidly.

De Grette.
The view on Kyiv (1849)
The National Art
Museum of Ukraine

The Magdeburg Law
Column (1802-1808,
archt. A. Melensky)

Intercession Church (1889) of Intercession Monastery

Empress Elisaveta Petrovna carriage given to Metropolitan Rafail (Zaborovsky). 18ᵗʰ c., The National Museum of History of Ukraine

Resurrection rotunda-church (1824) at St. Flor's Convent

The Monastery of the Presentation of the Mother of God and the mosaic image of Mother of God on the Church of the presentation of the Mother of God

Defensive wall around the Near Caves. On the right there is a well of Rev. Anthonius, the founder of Pechersk Lavra

The population increased dramatically as well (71 thousand people in 1865, 626 thousand people in 1914).

In 1898, under the initiative of sugar produsers the *Tereschenko*, the *Brodsky*, and counts *Bobrynsky*, **Kyiv Polytechnic Institute** (KPI) was opened after the sample of Zurich and Munich ones. By 1901 – for the strikingly short period – the whole campus was built: 6 huge Neo-Gothic buildings. Nowadays KPI is one of the largest technical universities in the world (about 50 thousand students study here). The first exams were graded by *D. Mendeleyev*. An outstanding economist and philosopher *S. Bulgakov*, mechanics *V. Kirpichev* (chancelor) and *S. Timoshenko* (1878-1972, the founder of the School of Technical Mechanics in the USA), bridge designer *Ye. Paton*, painter *M. Pimonenko* were among the lecturers. Air engineering was given by *N. de Launay*, a descendant of Bastille governor. He founded Kyiv Air Navigation Association and trained *G. Adler, F. Anders, D. Hryhorovych, V. Iordan,* brothers *Kasyanenko, A. Mikulin.* Kyivan *Dmitry Hryhorovych* (1883-1938) studied at the KPI and the University of Liège (Belgium). In 1913, he designed the first in the Russian Empire hydroplane M-1, and the following year the famous flying boat, the M-5, then the first in Russia hydroplane fighter M-11. In 1930 he co-created with *Polikarpov* the famous fighter I-5. Future founder of American helicopter engineering Kyivan *Igor Sikorsky* (1889-1972) assembled his first aircraft in KPI workshops. In 1913 he created the biggest plane in the world, 'Russian Warrior', and the first world's passenger aircraft 'Ilia Muromets Kyivsky'. In 1913 *P. Nesterov* looped the loop on *Nieuport IV*

for the first time in the world at Syrets Airfield of Kyiv. Now, this aerobatics is actually called 'Loop of Nesterov'. *Petr Nesterov* is buried at Syrets Cemetery in Kyiv.

The first electric tram in the Russian Empire began to run in 1892 in Kyiv, and in 1905 the first funicular (cable car) was built.

In 1892 the City Merchant's Assembly building was opened. Nowadays it is used by the Philharmonic Society. Its concert hall has excellent acoustics. Many famous musicians, composers and singers, such as *Tchaikovsky, Rakhmaninov , Shaliapin, Skriabin, Sobinov, Glie're, Horowitz,* and many others, performed on its stage. The Pope *John Paul II* met Kyivites here in 2001.

In 1898 the Solovtsov Theatre opened its doors. Now it is known as the **Ivan Franko National Academic Drama Theatre**. In front of the theatre, at 5 Franko Square, there is a building of the former Kyiv Gymnasium No. 8, which was built in 1897. *Sergei (Serge) Lifar,* the future premier danseur and choreographer of the Paris Opera Ballet, studied there. Love of Kyiv remains for all

Reconstructed St. Michael's Golden-Domed Cathedral (12th, 18th, 20th cc.)

The House of Peter I (late 17th – early 18th cc.)

Kyiv Polytechnical Institute (1898)

Memorial plaque to the aircaft designer I. Sikorsky

The National Bank of Ukraine (1902, 1934)

Kyivites till the end of their lives wherever destiny leads them. Thus in Sainte Genevieve du Bois near Paris the laconic epitaph 'Serge Lifar de Kiev' is carved on his tombstone.

In 1901 the Opera Theatre opened its doors to spectators. It was built in the French Renaissance style and seated 1628 persons. Many famous touring and Kyiv artists, such as *Leonid Sobinov, Fiodor Shaliapin, Mattia Battistini,* and *Anatoly Solovyanenko,* performed on its stage.

The rapid development of Kyiv was interrupted by the Civil War. In the course of three years (1918-1920), power in Kyiv changed eighteen times. The city became an arena of bloody battles. So many forces tried to conquer the city: the White, the Red, the Germans, the Poles, various forest gangs, Ukrainian national forces of various political platforms. It is impossible to mention them all.

For a short time Kyiv became the capital of the independent Ukrainian People's Republic (UNR), which was headed by

Mykhaylo Hrushevsky. During the Hetmanat time (april - december 1918) Ukraine was recognised as a nation by thirteen countries. Hetman *Pavlo Skoropadsky* established the Ukrainian Academy of Sciences. *Volodymyr Vernadsky* became its president; *Agathangel Krymsky* became its scientific secretary. *Skoropadsky* also established the library of the Academy of the Sciences, which had 1 million books. It contains 15 million units now and houses the depositary of the UN.

In the 1930ˢ the war against religion resulted in the barbarous destruction of many churches and monuments of architecture and arts. The most valuable among these were destroyed **St. Michael's Golden-Domed Cathedral** with its unique 11ᵗʰ-century mosaics and frescoes, as well as Epiphany Cathedral of Bratsky Monastery. St. Michael's Golden-Domed Cathedral and its bell-tower were rebuilt and redecorated with new murals at the end of the 20ᵗʰ c. Only a small number of buildings of **Bratsky Monastery** has preserved, and a restored Kyiv-Mohyla Academy (established in 1631) is located there now.

In the late 1930ˢ there were also plans to blow up **St. Sophia of Kyiv**. It was saved only owing to the intercession of the President of France who reminded *Stalin* that it was a French shrine as well, since the daughter of *Yaroslav the Wise* had built this cathedral and became the Queen of France. *Stalin*, who was negotiating the creation of a union with France and Great Britain against fascist Germany at that time, listened to the words of the President. In this way St. Sophia had been saved.

It was not just monuments and churches that suffered in

A self-portrait of Taras Shevchenko (1840)

Kiev. A Chain bridge (photo of the early 20ᵗʰ c., NAMU)

Park Bridge (1904), known as 'Devil's Bridge', or 'The Bridge of Lovers'

The funicular (1905)

the 1930ˢ. With clear evidence these years are called the years of 'shot renaissanse' and Holodomor (great famine of 1932 – 1933) in Ukraine. The most brilliant Ukrainian intelectuals, as well as many clergymen, were executed or imprisoned in labour camps.

These dark times in Kyiv's history were followed by even more terrible times – the fascist invasion. The heroic defence of the city lasted for 72 days. But the city could not hold out forever, and the two-year occupation began.

In the summer of 1942 players from the 'Dynamo Kyiv' football club won a match against a combined team of 'Luftwaffe' German fascist soldiers by five to three. After the game, which became known in history as the 'match of death', four football players of the 'Dynamo' team were executed.

The whole world knows about the tragedy at **Babi Yar** ('Old woman's ravine'). On September 29, 1941, during the fascist occupation of Kyiv, all Jews of the city were ordered under the threat of execution to gather at Melnykova Street next to the Jewish cemetery. Afterwards the soldiers started hounding them with dogs and ordered them to take off all their clothes. After this the victims were driven with truncheons far into the woods and were shot with machine guns at the edge of the steep. The wounded and those who were alive fell down into the Yar (ravine) while the dead fell on top of them. In the course of just two days, the 29ᵗʰ and the 30ᵗʰ of September, 33,771 people were killed and buried alive. This tragedy of Jewish and Ukrainian peoples is described in the novel 'Babi Yar' by Kyiv writer *Anatoliy Kuznetsov*. Overall more than a hundred thousand Jews were killed, as well as dozens of thousands of Ukrainians, Russians, and representatives of other nationalities. A seven candle **'Menorah' memorial** was erected near the site of the executions on the 50ᵗʰ anniversary of the tragedy. A path of sorrow leads to it from the former Jewish cemetery, and every year on the 29ᵗʰ of September it is used for a mourning procession to Babi Yar.

There were two other concentration camps in Kyiv besides Babi Yar. In one of them alone, **Darnytsky**, about 50,000 prisoners of war were executed. More than 100,000 people were taken from Kyiv for forced labour in Germany. On the 6ᵗʰ of November, 1943, Kyiv was liberated as a result of a heroic assault across the Dnieper River and fierce battles. These events are described in detail in **the National Museum of the History of the Great Patriotic War**.

The following figures show the scale of losses in Kyiv. In 1940, before the war, the population in Kyiv was 930,000 people, while after the liberation, in 1943, only 180,000 people remained. Only in the mid-1950ˢ Kyiv started to recover from the wounds inflicted by the war.

This is the time splendid samples of Soviet architecture date to: **National ExpoCentre of Ukraine** in Holosiyiv (1958, by *V. Orekhov, I. Mezentsev, A. Stanislavsky*, et al.) and **Khreschatyk**. The street part demolished during the war was built up with a new ensemble (1948-1957, by *A. Vlasov, A. Dobrovolsky, V. Yelizarov*, et al.), while the street itself was widened up to 100 m and got a boulevard as decoration. The buildings were finished with ceramics, red and grey granite and lavishly decorated with Soviet symbols. The same time the first all-welded bridge in the world was built over the Dnieper. It was named after its creator *E. Paton* (1953,

The main building of
T. Shevchenko National
University (1843)

The monument to
M. Hrushevsky
(1998, archt. M. Kyslyi)

The Teacher's House

The view on Kyiv-Pechersk
Lavra from Pechersk
Landscape Park

The Museum of the History
of the Great Patriotic War.
The gallery of the heroes
of the front

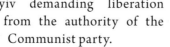

1543 m long). Pedestrian bridge (1957, 480 m long, 26 m high over the water, eng. *V. Kireyenko, L. Homin,* et al.) – spanned the right bank and Trukhaniv island with beaches and entertainment area. The 'Aviant' corporation located in Kyiv manufactures famous 'AN' airplanes, including the biggest airplanes in the world the AN-22 'Antey', the AN-124 'Ruslan', and the AN-225 'Mriya'.

During the 1960^s and 1970^s Kyiv became a powerful scientific centre of the USSR with distinguished scientists, such as *V. Hlushkov, B. Paton, M. Amosov,* and *O. Antonov.* Institutes of cybernetics, electric welding, ultra-hard materials, and others were at the leading edge of their fields in the scientific world. The second computing machine (ECM) in the world was created in Kyiv.

However, the period of stagnation had a pernicious effect on life in Kyiv, and the national liberation movement 'Rukh' ('Movement') began to gain strength. In 1989-1991 hundreds of thousands of Kyivites led by 'Rukh' went into the streets of Kyiv demanding liberation from the authority of the Communist party.

On the 24th of August, 1991, the Ukrainian Parliament (Verkhovna Rada, i.e. Supreme Council) proclaimed the Declaration of Independence of Ukraine, which was confirmed by the all-Ukrainian referendum on the 1st of December, 1991. Kyiv becomes the capital of the independent state.

The epicenter of the peaceful bourgeois Orange Revolution was in Khreschatyk and Maidan Nezalezhnosti from November 22 to December 8, 2004. A tent town was arranged here.

*Orange Revolution.
Camp on Khreschatyk (2004)*

*The monument to the victims
of Holodomor (great famine)
in 1932-1933*

*Babi Yar. The 'Menora'
monument (1991, by
Yu. Paskevych, A. Levich, et al.)*

*The 'Motherland' monument
(by V. Borodai,
V. Yelizarov, et al.)*

*The grave of artist
N.K. Pimonenko on
Lukyanovsky cemetery*

*The monument to the children
killed in Babi Yar in 1941
(2001, by V. Medvedev,
R. Kukharenko,
Yu. Melnychuk)*

Citizens of Ukraine were demanding the abolition of clan privileges, rule of law, and freedom of speech. The Kyivans made a decisive contribution into its victory and the election of *Victor Yuschenko* the President of Ukraine. But revolution leaders deceived hopes of Ukrainians. President *V. Yuschenko* and his former teammate *Yulia Timoshenko* started fighting for power and control over the national resources, the laws were completely ignored, nepotism throve, and corruption grew. This fight threw Ukraine into the severest economic crisis. As a result, *Victor Yanukovich* won the presidency in 2010.

'March of Millions' on Khreschatyk on December 8th, 2013

Hrushevskoho Street in the midst of conflict.

In the background – 'Berkut' fighters blocked the street

Yanukovich started preparation of the Ukraine–EU Association Agreement, but in parallel commenced establishing a mighty corruption vertical. He enhanced 'corporate ridership' in favour of his family. As a result of renunciation of the Ukraine–EU Association EUROMAIDAN started in Kyiv. With the police forces used for the EUROMAIDAN crackdown on November 30th 2013, a new bourgeois revolution of Dignity for democracy and European values has started.

On December 8th March of the Millions was held in Kyiv – over 500 000 Kyivers came protesting to Khreschatyk. But *Yanukovich* ignored them. Reacting on this, ultra-radical forces

joined the protest actions, and the fighting conflicts in Hrushevckoho Street caused the first victims. Yanukovich's unwillingness to lose the power resulted in tragedy. On February 18th when the Maidan was attacked by the BERKUT police unit, the House of Trade Unions where head quarters of radical groups were, was burnt down, that was followed on February 20th with the Institutska Street tragedy, when snipers-provokers shot down both protesters and BERKUT soldiers. Over a hundred were killed, and about 1000 injured during the protest actions in Kyiv. *Yanukovich* escaped from the country, and Kyiv started – slowly but surely – coming back to the peaceful life.

The path of memory lined with carnations in honor of the 'Heavenly Hundred'. This name is given to killed participants of actions against corrupt regime of Yanukovich

After the battle. Maidan Nezalezhnosti

Kyiv–the Capital of Ukraine

The Administration of the President of Ukraine

Kyiv City Council Hall

The Verkhovna Rada (Parliament) of Ukraine. Above: The main entrance hall. The plafond is decorated with 'Ukraine in Blossom' painted panel

The Cabinet of Ministers of Ukraine

The capital of Ukraine was moved from Kharkiv to Kyiv in June 1934. Magnificent administrative buildings were being erected in 1935-1939. 3-storeyed buildings of the military district headquarters at 11 Bankova Street, which house the **Administration of the President of Ukraine** today, were added (archt. *S. Hrihoriev*).

The 10-storeyed **building of the Cabinet of Ministers** (archt. *I. Fomin*, assisted by *P. Abrosimov*) has a total volume of 235 thousand cubic meters. The main façade is decorated with Corinthian order columns. The lower storeys are faced with Tulchyn labradorite, while the socle is revetted with polished granite. **The building of Verkhovna Rada of Ukraine** (by *V. Zabolotny*) harmonizes with Mariinsky Park landscape. Its façade is decorated with sculptural groups (sculp. *V. Znoba*). The session hall (650 sq. m, 1300 seats) is roofed with a glass dome. A semi-circular block was attached to the building at the side of City Park in 1945-1947.

The building at 36 Khreschatyk str., which houses the **Kyiv City Council Hall** (1957, by *A. Vlasov, A. Zavarov, A. Malinovsky*), has an area of 100 thousand sq. m and a meeting hall for 120 seats. The blue-yellow Ukraine's flag was raised for the first time over the City Council Hall in 1990.

Newly-erected buildings on the left bank.
On the left - Paton Bridge

'Pivdenny' (South) railway terminal

Boryspil International Airport. Terminal D

Business-center 'Parus' and multifunctional complex
'Gulliver'

The TV tower in Syrets

New area Novopecherski Lipki

Present-day Kyiv

Present-day Kyiv is the largest cultural, scientific, industrial and sports centre of Eastern Europe. The population of the city is 2.74 million and the area is 839 sq. km. It stretches for 42 km from north to south along the picturesque banks of the Dnieper and for 42 km from east to west as well. Kyiv is divided into ten administrative districts.

Kyiv receives its visitors at international **'Boryspil' airport** and local **'Zhulyany' airport**. The largest passenger **railway station (Kyiv-Passenger)** is equipped according to the most exacting requirements and consists of two buildings: an old constructivist building (built in 1927-1932, reconstructed in 2001) and a new ultra-modern building of **'Southern Station'**, constructed in 2001.

Travellers can also arrive in Kyiv at **River Station** located in the centre of Kyiv at the edge of Kyiv's historical area, **Podil**. From here it is possible to take a fascinating stroll along the Dnieper through Kyiv and admire captivating landscapes.

Visitors can also arrive in the city by bus at **Central Bus Terminal**. Those who prefer to travel by car can stop in numerous motels and at auto camp sites.

Cultural life in Kyiv is extremely varied. The city has very ancient musical and theatre traditions. One can see performances of minstrels and musicians depicted on 11th-century frescoes in **St. Sophia of Kyiv**. Music in Kyiv was taught as early as the Kyivan Rus period. *Anna*, the granddaughter of *Yaroslav the Wise*, opened a school where singers were trained in 1086. At the present time Kyiv has deservedly acquired the reputation of a great theatre and music centre. The Kyiv Ballet and the opera company tour worldwide,

Obolon is the one of the best residential neighbourhoods in Kyiv. Its development started in 1973. In Obolon there is a yacht club and a golf club

Obolon Embankment with the park of sculptures
In front – sculpture of the Frog Princess
(sculp. A. Shamshura)

The monument to the Archistratigus Michael – the patron saint of Kyiv
(2000, sculp. M. Znoba)

Santiago-de-Chile Square. Commemorative sign with condor and guanaco – the symbols of Chile
(2001, sculp. M. Znoba)

Obolon Embankment

and such opera singers as *D. Hnatyuk, E. Miroshnychenko, A. Solovyanenko,* tenor *Yu. Kiporenko-Damansky,* baritone *V. Hryshko* have obtained worldwide recognition. A famous conductor *Volodymyr Kozhukhar* led the Kyiv Opera.

T. Shevchenko National Opera and its interior

Besides academic theatres there are many small theatres and theatre-studios in Kyiv. Many of them are well-known abroad. For example, the Kyiv 'Theater on Podil', of which *V. Malakhov* is the director, and the 'Suziria' Dramatic Art Studio (art director *O. Kuzhelny*) have repeatedly received prizes at the most prestigious theatrical festivals. **Kyiv Conservatoire** (National Music Academy) was founded in 1913. It is located at the corner of Khreschatyk and Horodetskoho streets. At the conservatoire there is a concert hall, where well-known international competitions take place. Among the graduates of the conservatoire are such well-known singers as *D. Hnatyuk; E. Miroshnychenko; L. Rudenko; A. Solovyanenko; N. Kondratyuk; E. Yarotska;* composers *L. Revutsky; B. Lyatoshynsky; E. Stankovych* (who is in the world top ten of composers); and the conductor *V. Sirenko.* The outstanding conductor *Stefan Turchak* taught in the conservatoire. The renowned tenor *Ivan Kozlovsky* studied in Kyiv.

A memorial tablet to Vladimir Horowitz on the house, where he was born

The famous piano virtuoso *Volodymyr Horowitz* was born in 1903 in Kyiv in the house at M. Kotsyubynskoho Street, No. 12. An annual international competition of young pianists in his memory is held in Kyiv. An annual international festival of classical music 'Kyiv Music Fest' takes place as well in the city.

Alexander Dovzhenko National Film Studio is situated in Kyiv. Famous film directors *Sergey Paradzhanov, Alexander Dovzhenko,* and *Vasily Bykov* have worked there. *Sergey Paradzhanov* has shot his famous 'Shades of Forgotten Ancestors'(1964) at this studio. International festival "Gogolfest" is becoming popular every year.

Kyiv State Academic Puppet Theatre

Founded in 1927 by *A. Solomarsky*, People's Artist of Ukraine, and *I. Deyeva*. The theatre is famous for the top artistry of puppeteers. In 1991 the theatre initiated the International Puppet Theatre Festival attracting to Kyiv companies from many countries of Europe, Japan, China, Russia. The theatre building designed by architects *V. Yudin* and *O. Yudina* as a fairy tale castle was constructed in 2005. Two halls may seat 296 and 100 people, correspondingly.

Statues of favourite children's tale characters: **Buratino** and **Pierro** (by *H. Savchenko*), **Malvina** and **Artemon** (by *V. Primakov*), **Papa Carlo, Thumbelina, Kotyhoroshko** (all by *T. Tsiupa, I. Hlukhenky*), **Bremen Musicians** (by *H. Savchenko*). The theatre interiors are painted with splendid pictures of Ukrainian fairy-tales' characters (by *K. Lavrov,* et al.), decorated with ceramics (*B. Danilov*)

and marvellous candelabra (*M. Ralko*). The fairy-tale atmosphere impresses even more thanks to a huge aquarium; small gnomes mining treasures; a collection of antique theatre puppets; and a floor lavishly incrusted with granite and timber (*O. Yudina*).

The Puppet Theatre and 'Thumbelina' musical fountain (2005)

Theatre interiors, decorated with paintings by the fairy tale 'Pan Kotsky' (artist K. Lavrov)

Sculptures of Pierro, Malvina with Artemon, Buratino, and Kotyhoroshko (below)

Olexander Shovkovsky

Andriy Shevchenko

The monument to Valery Lobanovsky (2003), the coach of Dynamo Kyiv football team and the national football team of Ukraine (2003, by V. Filatov)

Sport Kyiv

Kyiv has been known for its sport traditions for ages. It was here that the First All-Russian Olympic Games took place in 1913. The sport most popular among the Kyivans is football (soccer). DYNAMO Kyiv is permanently on the list of top rated European teams. Trained at DYNAMO Sport School for Children and Youth, *Oleg Blokhin* and *Andrii Shevchenko*, born in Kyiv, became the best football players of Europe in 1975 and 2004, correspondingly. DYNAMO Kyiv revealed a talent of *Igor Belanov* from Odesa who was awarded with Ballon d'Or in 1976. The skillful DYNAMO goalkeeper *Alexander Shovkovsky* from Kyiv played brilliantly at the 2006 World Football Cup, and guaranteed the Ukrainian national team getting into the Last Eight, not conceding a goal in the penalty shootout.

A beach football is also popular in the capital, especially in the Hydropark. Kyiv teams are leaders in Ukraine, and in 2010 the Ukrainian national beasal team, becoming first in Europe, was qualified for 2011 World Cup final.

Basketball is ranked high in Kyiv, too. The rivalling basketball clubs –BUDIVELNYK and KYIV – are well known in Europe.

Kyiv offers excellent conditions for yachting, canoeing and kayaking. *Valentyn Mankin* – a legendary alumnus of Kyiv sailing sports division – was born in Kyiv in 1938. He became the yachtsman in the world who won Olympic gold in three different categories – Finn (1968), Tempest (1972), and Star (1980). At the 1976 Olympic Games he won the silver medal in Tempest Class. Champion of Europe in 1973, 1978, 1979. In 1988 *Valentin Mankin* became a chief coach of Italian Sailing Federation and trained a lot of world-class yachtsmen. In 1967 Cruiser Yacht-Club was founded in Kyiv (http://yachtclub.kiev.ua). Kyivans *Rodion Luka* and *Georgiy Leonchuk* won silver medals of the 2004 Olympic Games, the 2005 World Cup, and got Grand Prix at Volvochampionsrace in 2006 on the 49er sailing dinghy. In 2009 the water area of Kyiv Water Reservoir hosted the First WindMaster Regatta – racings in sportboat and racer classes within the European Cup.

Kyivans have always been riveted by the sky. Here the aviation designing school appeared at the beginning of 20th c. on the base of Kyiv Polytechnic Institute. Everybody who wants to balloon into the sky may address the Ballooner Club 'By Balloon Over Ukraine' (http://www.nashare.in.ua) as well as go in for gliding at AERO Paragliding Club (http://aero-kiev.com). At CHAYKA Airfield one may be trained to bail out and do this from AN28 Aircraft, height of 4,200 m (http://www.dropzone.kiev.ua).

Since ancient times wrestling has been popular in Kyiv. Kyiv legendary warriors – *Ilia Muromets, Kirill Kozhemiaka,* and *Alesha Popovich* – are well known. Before the revolution Krutikov's Circus, with 2000 seat audience, was extremely popular, and it was completely full during wrestler performances. The USSR 1ˢᵗ Greco-Roman Championship was held in Kyiv in 1924. *Hryhoriy Hamarnyk* from Kyiv became a world champion in 1955, and *Ivan Bohdan* won the Olympic gold in Rome in 1960. *Alexander Medved* three times became an Olympic champion in free style wrestling (1964, 1968, 1972) in different weight categories, including the absolute one, and seven times won the world championship. *Alexander Kolchinsky* was a two-time Olympic champion (1976, 1980), and *Alexander Zakharuk* – a five-time champion of Europe.

Grand opening of the 70,000 seat Olympic Stadium in Kyiv (October 8, 2011)

Boxing and kickboxing are popular in Kyiv, too. The famous brothers *Klichko* started their carrier in Kyiv with kickboxing. It was in 1991 when *Alexey Nechayev* (weight of 54kg), *Viktor Doroshenko* (weight of 81kg) and *Vitaliy Klichko* (weight +91kg) from Kyiv won three of 4 gold medals in Paris. In 1992 the head office of All-Eurasian Kickboxing Federation was opened in Kyiv.

Obolon. International Sailing Regatta 'Hetman Cup' – 2016

A lot of Kyivans are fond of dances of all kinds, artistic and rhythmic sportive gymnastics. There are hundreds of dancing schools, clubs and studios in Kyiv. One of them is Kyiv School for Rhythmic Sportive Gymnastics of *Albina* and *Irina Deriuginys* known in the whole world.

Famous Kyivans

Nikolai Berdyaev
(1874-1948)

A house, where
K. Malevich was born
(has not remained,
fig. by A. Pavlov)

K. Malevich. Black
Square (1915)

Leon Bakst. Vaslav
Nijinsky in the
ballet Afternoon of a
Faun (1912)

"The Gold Shoe" of
Serge Lifar

Kyiv has given the world many outstanding people. They were formed in the amazing atmosphere of the city. Here we describe only some of them.

In 1874 in Lypky, in the heart of Pechersk, a future philosopher *Nikolai Berdyaev* was born into an aristocratic family. Among his ancestors was Novorossiysk Governor-General *N. Berdyaev*, a defender of liberties of Cossack Ataman of the Don Army *M. Berdyaev*, Kiev vice-governor (1838 – 1844) Prince *S. Kudashev*, grandmother of Count *Choiseul-Gouffier* family. *Berdyaev's* family was also related to Countess *Maria Branickaya* (Princess *Sapieha*), who owned luxurious estate "Alexandria" in Bila Tserkva. Since 1924 *Berdyaev* lived in Clamart, near Paris. His works were devoted to individual liberty and a sense of creativity. He had a significant impact on the development of French existentialism and personalism. In 1947, *Berdyaev* was elected an honorary doctor of theology (Honoris causa), University of Cambridge (Great Britain).

In Kyiv, Podil, in a wealthy Jewish family, was born another famous philosopher *Lev Shestov* (Schwarzman, 1866 – 1938, Paris).

Vaslav Nijinsky (1890 – 1950) was born into the family of a Kiev dancer Thomas Nijinsky, owner of his own ballet troupe. He became a leading member of *Diaghilev's* Russian Ballet. In 1912 he amazed Paris with ballets "The Afternoon of a Faun", in which he acted as a choreographer and main performer, and "The Rite of Spring". He was buried in the cemetery of Montmartre in Paris. In his sister's *Bronislava* Kyiv studio studied the art of dance *Serge Lifar* (1905 – 1986). He was born in Kiev, Tarasivska street in a wealthy family of a clerk *Michael Lifar*. His mother *Sophia Marchenko* came from a Cossack family and owned an estate near Kanev. In 1922 *B. Nijinskaya* emigrated to Paris and invited *Lifar*. Soon *Lifar* became an idol of the Parisians. In 1924 he headed the ballet troupe of the "Grand Opera" and staged here more than 200 ballets. He founded the Paris University of Choreography and was the founder of a new direction in the ballet – "neoclassicism". He was awarded the highest ballet award – "The Golden Shoe" and Golden Medal of the City of Paris.

Mikhail Bulgakov was born in 1891 in Podil (on Vozdvizhenka) in the family of a professor of the Kyiv Theological Academy. He graduated from Kiev University (Medical School). *Mikhail Bulgakov's* works, tied with Kyiv by thousands of threads, are the best to tell about an outstanding writer.

Famous actress *Milla Jovich* (Mila Dzhovovich) was born on the 17th of December, 1975 in Kyiv Borshchagovka (str. Gnat Yura, 10A) in a family of a famous Soviet actress *Galina Loginova* and a doctor from Montenegro *Bogi Dzhovovich*. In 1979 she moved with her parents in the U.S., but surely, according to *Freud*, it were her early years that laid Milla's world view.

Milla Jovich

Oleg Blokhin

Irina Deriugina

Folk Dance Ensemble of Igor Moiseyev, Kyiv, 2010

Oleg Blokhin was born in 1952 in Kyiv, Chokolivka. He studied at the FC "Dynamo" (Kyiv) junior school, and soon won a firm place in the main part of the football team. He won the Golden Ball (1975). Led by him, Ukrainian team became a quarterfinalist of the World Cup 2006. *Irina Deriugina* was born in 1958 in Kyiv in the sports family. She became twice the absolute world champion in artistic gymnastics (1977, 1979). She had a tremendous influence on the development of artistic gymnastics in Ukraine. She organized the annual international competition in artistic gymnastics "Deriugina Cup." in Kyiv.

An outstanding artist and a literary critic *Maximilian Kiriyenko-Voloshin* was born in 1877 in Kyiv in the family of a lawyer. His house in Koktebel (Crimea) has become a pilgrimage site of poets, writers and cultural figures. *Voloshin* died here in 1932.

Igor Moiseyev was born in Kyiv in 1906 into a noble family of a lawyer *Alexander Moiseyev* and milliner *Anna Gran*. In 1937 he created the country's first professional folk dance ensemble and has developed a unique method of creative interpretation of folklore, combining the techniques of folk and professional art. His dance theater impressed his contemporaries so much, that it became the first folk dance ensemble to be honored to perform at the Paris Grand Opera and Milan's La Scala in 1966. A special medal "Les triomphesde "Les danses poloviennes" de Igor Moiseyev" was struck in Paris in honor of his ballet "Polovetsian Dances". *Moiseyev* died in 2007.

Another famous Kyivans aircraft designers *Igor Sikorsky* and *Dmitry Grigorovich*, politician *Golda Meir*, pianist *Vladimir Horowitz, Kazimir Malevich* were mentioned above. Kyiv was also a birth place of sculptor *Alexander Arkhipenko*, a founder of 'archipenture', movable painting art.

A memorial tablet to M. Voloshin on the house, where he was born (Shevchenko bul., No.22-24, sculp. M. Rapay)

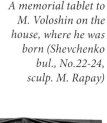

Walks through Kyiv

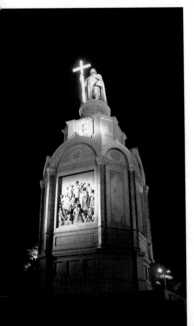

St. Michael's Golden-Domed Monastery

The monument to Prince Volodymyr Equal to the Apostles, the Baptiser of Kyivan Rus

Christmas at St. Sophia Square

Certainly, the first walk should begin on Volodymyrska Street from **the Golden gates** (built in 1017-1024), the main entrance to so called 'Yaroslav's town'. In 1983 the Golden gates were restored according to scientific assumptions. Inside the pavilion there are authentic ruins of the gates from the time of *Yaroslav the Wise* (1019-1054). A museum is opened here, as well as an observation platform from which it is possible to imagine the might of the rampart that used to surround ancient Kyiv. The rampart extended for 3.5 km, and had a base width of 30 meters and a height of up to 16 meters. The rampart was surrounded by a ditch. The total area of the ancient town was 60 hectares. Yaroslav's rampart ran along the present-day street of the same name Yaroslaviv Val (i.e. 'Yaroslav's rampat') up to **Lvivska Square**, where Lviv gates were located. At 15 Yaroslaviv Val Street in a courtyard there is a building where *Igor Sikorsky*, the future famous aircraft designer and the founder of American helicopter engineering, spent his childhood and adolescent years. On the opposite side from the Golden gates the rampart went down to the area of **Independence Square** where Lyadski gates were located. (At that place there is an arch decorated in baroque now). Then the rampart went upwards along **Kostyolna Street** and around **St. Michael's Square** merged into the rampart of 'Volodymyr's town'. To the right of the Golden gates at the corner of the Volodymyrska Street and **Prorizna Street** stands a magnificent building (**No. 39**) constructed in 1901. A confectionary store called 'Marquisa' mentioned in *Bulgakov's* 'The White Guards' used to be located there.

At **35 Volodymyrska Street** a former private residence of the architect *A. Beretti* (1848) stands. And in front of it, in building **No. 36**, was the 'Prague' hotel where in 1916-1918 *Jaroslav Hašek* lived. It was Kyiv where 'The Good Soldier Švejk in Captivity', which gave birth to 'The Good Soldier Švejk and His Fortunes', had came to light. At the corner of Volodymyrska and Irynynska streets one can see a marking outlining the location of the ancient **St. Irene's church** named in honour of the patron saint of the wife of Prince Yaroslav the Wise, *Irene (Ingegerd Olofsdotter)*, daughter of the king of Sweden. Further along, the street goes into **St. Sophia Square**, where through the bell tower is the main entrance to the

St. Sophia courtyard. This area has now been declared a preserve and was designated by UNESCO as World Heritage Site in 1990.

The magnificent 76-meter-high bell tower together with **St. Sophia of Kyiv** creates a baroque ensemble of amazing beauty. A 13-ton bell cast in 1705 still hangs from the second tier of the bell tower. On the preserve's territory there is **a refectory church** called **Warm Sophia, residence of the Metropolitan** (1722-1730), consistory (the 'Khlibnya' ('Bread Room') exhibition hall). The main entrance used to lead to the residence of the Metropolitan through majestic gate called the **Gate of Zaborovsky**. At the centre of this assemblage is the most unique structure of ancient Rus architecture, the magnificent 19-domed **St. Sophia Cathedral** (which was laid in 1011). It was named after the Cathedral of St. Sophia in Constantinople (from the Greek word 'sophia' which means 'wisdom'). It was constructed as the main metropolitan church of Kyivan Rus in honour of the victory of the ancient Rus' army over pagan nomads and for the glorification of Christianity. One third of all the paintings which adorned the church in ancient Rus' times, that is 260 sq. m of mosaics and about 3,000 sq. m of frescoes from the 11th c., is preserved inside the cathedral. Besides 11th-century mosaics and frescoes on the cathedral walls one can see works of artists from 17th to 19th centuries. At the zenith of the dome in a medallion design there is a mosaic image of Christ the Pantocrator, and around him there are four figures of archangels, one of which is a mosaic from the 11th c., and the others were painted in oil by *M. Vrubel* in 1884. One hundred and seventy seven shades of enamel blue were used for making the mosaics of the cathedral.

In the apse in all its magnificence appears the majestic six-meter figure of the **Mother of God 'Oranta'** (i.e. praying). This image is called the **'Inviolable Wall'**, as the wall on which the Mother of God is represented is indestructible and is preserved in its original condition. It seems as if the divine power protects it. Inhabitants of Kyiv believe that this cathedral and the Mother of God 'Oranta' in the centre of it are protectors of the city, and as long as the cathedral stands nothing will threaten the city.

St. Sophia Cathedral. The altar apse. In the centre – 'Inviolable wall' with the mosaic of the Mother of God 'Oranta'

The view on St. Sophia Cathedral from above

Memorial plaque to the writer Jaroslav Hašek

Standing in the cathedral, you feel an especially calming power. You are seized with tremors of devotion and a feeling of contact with eternity. If St. Sophia makes such an impression on modern, it is difficult even to imagine the feelings of the first visitors of the cathedral. The burial vault of great princes is found in the cathedral.

The **sarcophagus** of *Yaroslav the Wise* and his wife *Irene* is preserved in St. Sophia. The white marble sarcophagus was brought from Byzantium and was probably made as early as in the 7th to the 8th centuries. In the refectory church one can also see the 10th to the 11th century **sarcophagus** of *Princess Olha*, which has been brought here from Desyatynna Church.

On the first floor of St. Sophia there is a unique display of original mosaics and frescoes dating to the beginning of the 12th c. from St. Michael's Golden-Domed Cathedral. A majestic panoramic view of **St. Michael's Golden-Domed Cathedral** is revealed from St. Sophia Square, and in the foreground stands the **monument to Cossack Hetman Bohdan Khmelnytsky** (1881-1888).

Continuing the walk on Volodymyrska, on the right we pass the buildings of former provincial establishments known as '**Prisutstvennyye Myesta**', i.e. offices (1854-1857). A **fire tower**, which served as a lookout for suspicious smoke, ajoints to this building.

On the opposite side of Volodymyrska Street in building No. 16 (1879) used to be a **private hotel** where the artists *M. Vrubel* and *M. Nesterov* lived. The outstanding Ukrainian poet and human rights activist *Vasyl Stus* also worked here.

At the intersection of Volodymyrska and Velyka Zhytomyrska streets it is possible to see the red quartz outline of the **foundation of St. Sophia gates**, which in turn led into the **town of Volodymyr**, the most ancient part of Kyiv. At the beginning of Volodymyrska Street it is possible to find a memorial plaque at the site of the Grand Prince's Palace (10th c.), as well as remains of **pagan temples** (10th c.). While going up to the **National Museum of the History of Ukraine**, we will see the remains of the foundation of the most ancient Kyiv's stone temple, Desyatynna Church (998). Here Prince Volodymyr, the Baptiser of Rus, was buried. If you approach the edge of Starokyivska (i.e. 'Old Kyiv') hill, the incomparable view of the ancient areas of **Honchary** and **Kozhumyaki** as well as **Zamkova hill** will be revealed before you.

On the left rises **Dytynka hill**. It is here where lovers of meditation and members of spiritual societies come to carry out their activities. The hill is also revered by Kyiv artists. On the right the vistas of the Dnieper and the left bank open.

Memorial plaque to the musician and composer F. Liszt

Memorial plaque to the pilot Piotr Nesterov

Memorial plaque to the poet, composer, and actor A. Vertinsky

The Golden gates after the reconstruction

Going back to the beginning of Volodymyrska Street, we find ouselves before the outstanding creation of *B. Rastrelli*, **St. Andrew's Church**. It stands at the top of Andrew's hill. In the most ancient Russian chronicle, 'The Story of the Passing Years', the legend was written down that Andrew, the First-called Apostle, preaching Christianity, had spent the night on a slope by the Dnieper, and early in the morning climbed a hill (subsequently named Andrew's hill), erected a cross, and uttered to the people: 'On these hills divine grace will shine. There will be a great city, and God will erect many churches here'.

The annals inform that St. Andrew's monastery had already stood on this place in the 11th c. While staying in Kyiv in 1744, *Empress Elizabeth* placed the first stone in the foundation of the future St. Andrew's Church. The consecration of the church was held in 1767. The church is built in baroque and surprisingly harmonizes with the surrounding hilly area. During its construction it was necessary to resolve difficult problems in the development and strengthening of the foundation. A complex drainage system was created around the foundation. The height of the five-domed St. Andrew's Church together with the stylobate is 62 meters. The interior decoration of the church amazes one with its richness. It was tastefully and carefully carried out according to the design and drawings of the iconostasis made by *B. Rastrelli*. The best St. Petersburg's carvers created the iconostasis. The sketches for dome paintings and 25 icons for the iconostasis were created by Petersburg artist Ivan Yakovich Vishnyakov with his disciples. The works of the well-known Russian artist *A. Antropov* ('The Last Supper', 'The Assumption of The Mother of God', and altar paintings) are especially impressive. The interiors were decorated with pictures "Sermon of Apostle Andrew to the Scythians" (1847, by art. P. G. Borispolets) and "Choice of Faith by Prince Vladimir" (by art. I. L. Eggink).

The paintings in the church interact harmoniously with the wood carvings, and the gilding creates a unique play of light with a background of turquoise and purple colours. As a whole the refined appearance of the exterior together with the decoration of the interior of the church create a celebratory, cheerful mood.

From St. Andrew's Church begins **Andriivsky Descent** (i.e. St. Andrew's Descent, or Andriivsky Uzviz in Ukrainian), which winds between the Kyiv hills and ends in Podil.

Kyiv Days at Andriivsky Descent

Pages 50-51: St. Andrew's Church (1747-1753) and its interior

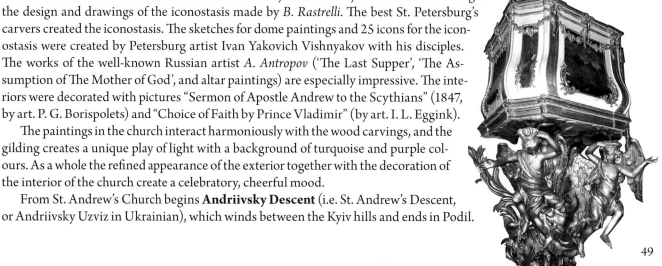

It is difficult to find any other street in the world which can be compared with Andriivsky Descent in its picturesque beauty. It was most probably because of this that the street was always so beloved by artists. Many well-known artists, sculptors, and writers lived here. The most famous of them was *Mikhail Bulgakov*. The little house at 13 Andriivsky Descent is called the **'House of Bulgakov'**. He lived in this house from 1906 to 1916 and from 1918 to 1919. And it is precisely this place where he set the heroes of his 'The White Guards' and 'The Days of the Turbins'. Now a museum is located there.

Andriivsky Descent is called Kyiv's Montmartre. It is a favoured place of artists, who gather here each year at the end of May during the opening of **'Kyiv Days'**. Then the street becomes a place of pilgrimage for tens of thousands of Kyivites and visitors to the capital. Concerts and art festivals are held here traditionally, and many picture galleries, souvenir shops, and antique dealers display their wares.

The sensuality which spreads over Kyiv, the contrasting play of sunlight, the gold of the domes, the light spots on buildings, and the relief contrasts of green hills were subsequently embodied in the surprising creativity of the genius painter, Kyivite *Kazimir Malevich*. He studied not far from here, in the Drawing School of N. Murashko at 47 Volodymyrska Street.

To the left of the street you can go up to the top of Zamkova hill by a winding **cast-iron staircase**. There you will get a picturesque view of St. Andrew's Church and a sweeping vista of the Dnieper in the distance. On the side of Honchary and Kozhumyaky areas you can see **Vozdvyzhenska Street**, where in ap wing (has not been preserved) of the building **No. l0** *Mikhail Bulgakov* was born. At the beginning of Vozdvyzhenska Street stands the **Church of the Exaltation of the Holy Cross** (1811-1841). There used to be a castle on Zamkova hill in the Middle Ages. Having taken a look at the steep incline of this hill, one will easily convince oneself of its impregnability. Archaeologists consider it was right here that the core of the city of Kyiv was situated. The cemetery of **St. Flor's Convent** is found on the northern side of Zamkova hill.

On the right side of Andriivsky Descent next to Bulgakov's house there is a building that Kyiv writer *Victor Nekrasov* romantically has nicknamed the '**Castle of Richard the Lion-Hearted**'. The building stands out for its gothic-like architectural style and monumental faHades decorated with elements typical of fortresses and castles. To the left of the building, a steep, twisting cast-iron staircase swoop you up to the top of **Uzdykhalny-tsya hill** – the most cherished lookout observation platform for Kyivites. From its eight a captivating view of **Podil** and **Obolon districts**, **Moscow Bridge**, **Voskresenka** and **Troyeschyna districts** opens. In good weather you can see the Desenka river which flows into the **Chortoryi channel**.

The monument to M. Bulgakov (2007, sculp. M. Reva)

The house of Mikhail Bulgakov. The author settled the Turbins family there ('The Days of the Turbins' and 'The White Guard')

Andriivsky Descent

The heroes of the classical hit movie 'After Two Hares' – Pronia Prokopivna and Holokhvastov (1999, sculp. W. Schur, V. Sivko)

The romantic mood which is created on the top of the mountain attracts couples in love who, dying from rapture, turn their eyes towards the unembraceable distance.

It is well-known that in every self-respecting historical city a **Lysa Hora** (Bald mountain) exists, where on sabbath the evil spirit is cast away. In Kyiv there were three such hills. The hill most beloved by witches was situated on the left bank in the vicinity of present-day **Voskresenka** district. Not only Kyivan witches, but also those from its neighbourhood came here flying over the Dnieper. But this hill vanished. The second one is called Yurkovytsya nowadays. The third historical Lysa Hora in Kyiv outskirts (near Vydubychi subway station) has a gloomier claim to fame. Its strong negative energy is well known not only in Kyiv, but in the whole Eastern Europe. If you want to feel yourself a hero of phantasmagoria as depicted in Bulgakov's 'The Master and Margarita', then stay on top of this hill at night. Here phantasmagoria becomes reality. At the same time it is not recommended for nervous people to visit Lysa Hora.

At night Andriivsky Descent looks much friendlier, but not less magical. From the top of Uzdykhalnytsya hill, the cupola of **St. Andrew's Church** steams, at the bottom, the evening lights in Podil twinkle, and all around the Kyivan hills perish in secret silence. Through the nightly silence the outlines of the trees turn into mythological beings, and it seems as right here a Bulgakov's Margarita will fly over you at any moment. At the bottom of Andriivsky Descent there is a unique **'Museum of One Street'** dedicated to the history of Andriivsky Descent. Here you can be absorbed into the atmosphere of the turn of the 20th c. and see the world through the eyes of the Artist.

Podil

It is best to start the stroll through Podil from **Kontraktova** (Contract) **Square**. This is the most ancient square in Podil, the old merchant town, which in the 19th c. became a part of Kyiv. This square is known since the time of Kyivan Rus. In 1132-1136 **the Church of the Mother of God Pyrohoscha** was built here. It is mentioned in the heroic epic 'The Lay of the Host of Igor'. This church was the most revered one in Podil. The magistrate of Podil held ceremonies and kept the town records here. The church was demolished in 1935, and in 1998 a new cathedral in the ancient Rus style was built at the same spot. In general, the square recreates the trading atmosphere of Podil at the end of the 18th – the beginning of the 19th c.

The harmony of the square is marred by a four-storey building in the pseudo-classical style built at the spot where the bell tower of Bratsky (Brotherhood) Monastery used to stand. The bell tower was demolished in 1930. The University of **Kyiv-Mohyla Academy**, which was reestablished in 1992, occupies this building now. It was the oldest institute of higher education in Kyiv. In 1632 *Petro Mohyla* combined Lavra and Brotherhood schools into Kyiv-Mohyla College. It received the rights and the title of academy in 1701, and in 1819 it was reorganized into Theological Academy.

Kyiv Academy was the most famous and prestigious learning centre of Eastern Europe. Students from not only Slavic, but also from Western European countries received a fundamental education here. During the course of several centuries Kyiv Academy was preparing the secular and clerical elite for the entire orthodox world.

The old building (1703-1740) together with **congregation Annunciation Church** (1732-1740) and the assembly hall has preserved till now. Philosophical debates and musical events took place here. Opposite this building stands **the monument** to the philosopher *Hryhoriy Skovoroda* (by *I. Kavaleridze*) who in 1738-1742 and 1744-1750 studied at the academy. *A. Bezborodko, A. Vedel, I. Hryhorovych-Barsky, A. Myloradovych, I. Samoylovych* studied there as well.

On the territory of the academy several unique 17th-19th-century buildings of destroyed **Bratsky Monastery** have preserved. Among them a **refectory with Holy Spirit Church** (17th-19th cc.) and a **sundial** are worth mentioning.

Bratsky Monastery. The Refectory with Holy Spirit Church (17th-19th cc.). On the right - the sundial

Intercession Church (1772) and the bell tower

The view on Podil

Memorial plaque to the Metropolitan P. Mohyla

Reconstructed Church of the Nativity of Jesus Christ. Taras Shevchenko coffin was placed in this church. On the right there is a former post station building (the 2ⁿᵈ half of the 19ᵗʰ c.)

St. Elijah's Church (1692)

Kontraktova Square. The bell tower of the former Greek St. Catherine's Monastery

The monument to Taras Shevchenko (1939, sculp. M. Manizer, archt. Ye. Levinson)

Pages 56-57: View on Podil Fountains on Rusanovka channel Pedestrian Bridge

In Kontraktova Square several buildings of Modern architecture stand out, as well as the structures of **Greek-Sinai St. Catherine's Monastery**, which was founded in 1748 by Greek colonists. Among the nearest sights deserving one's attention as well are **St. Flor's Convent** and the **Church of St. Nikolas Prytysk**. You also should see the little **house** built at the end of the 17ᵗʰ c. where, according to legend, *Peter the Great* stayed. Nowadays a museum is located there.

At l6A Spasska Street near Kontraktova Square there is an early 18ᵗʰ century building which Hetman *Ivan Mazepa* supposedly lived in. Nowadays **the Museum of Ukrainian Hetmans** is located here. Not far from the museum is **St. Nicolas' Naberezhny Church** (1772-1775) constructed in the Ukrainian baroque style. Next to it it stands a granite cross bearing an inscription in Ukrainian: 'To those who sacrificed their lives at the altar of Ukraine.'

A few steps away, the surprisingly cosy **St. Elijah's Church** named in honour of Elijah the Prophet stands. It was built in 1692 at the site where the oldest Christian church in Kyiv used to be located. In the year of 945, the representatives of Kyiv Prince *Igor* took an oath at the signing of the peace treaty with Byzantium there. **St. Elijah's Church** stands at Pochaynynska Street named in memory of the full-flowing river Pochayna, which in Kyivan Rus times used to fall into the Dnieper at this location.

Next to St. Elijah's Church there is the Dnieper quay. Scheduled boats, as well as tourist, hotel, and restaurant boats are moored here. Ноцит far away there is **River-boat Station**. Next to it there is Poshtova (Post) Square, which gets its name from the **post station** (1846), from where postal transportation began and mail coaches were sent out. Not far from the former post station there is a **Church of the Nativity of Christ**. On 6-7 May, 1861 the body of *Taras Shevchenko* was placed there. Then the casket was taken along today's Naberezhne Highway to the ship leaving to Kaniv from the station not far from present-day Metro Bridge.

Khreschatyk and Its Surroundings

Khreschatyk is a central street of Kyiv. The street got its name from a ravine with a small spring called Khreschaty that flew here before. From the bird's eye Khreschatyk looks like a cross. The street is only 1,300 meters long but it is well known far outside Kyiv. Khreschatyk is not only a business and administrative centre of the city – it is also the Kyivites' favourite place for entertainment and rest.

At the southern end of the street there is a **Bessarabsky Market** built in 1912 in Art Nouveau style. Centuries ago there was an open-air market here where Bessarabian farmers used to bring their products. Nowadays it is a central city market that offers products of very good quality.

In Bessarabka neighbourhood, at 5 Basseina Street, a girl *Golda* was born in the family of the carpenter *Itsko Mabovich*. Later she became the prime minister of Israel – *Golda Meir*. Around here, at 5 Velyka Vasylkivska Street, in 1887-1890 and in 1893-1905 a well-known Jewish writer *Sholem Aleichem* lived. While living in Kyiv he wrote his brilliant 'Tevye the Milkman'. In his works he described his beloved city of Kyiv under the fictitional name 'Yegupets' but left original names of Kyiv streets and cafes. There is a **monument to Sholem Aleichem** (by *V. Medvedev*) in Rohnidynska Street.

A new modern business centre with a hotel and shopping malls has been recently erected between Baseyna and Velyka Vasylkivska streets.

Across from Bessarabska Square a beautiful Shevchenko Boulevard decorated with two lines of Bolle's poplars goes up the hill. The boulevard starts with the **monument to Lenin** (by *S. Merkurov*) erected in 1946.

There is also a picturesque boulevard with famous Kyiv chestnuts on the odd side of Khreschatyk Street. Kyivites like to spend their free time here sitting on the benches chatting and drinking beer or lemonade. Khreschatyk is a street of open-air cafes and bars. You can find a lot of them in a quiet **Passage** that was built in 1913-1915.

In September, 1941 Soviet resistance fighters blew down most buildings in Khreschatyk where fascist occupiers' offices were accommodated. In the 1950ˢ a new socialist realism ensemble was raised on their sites, while the street was significantly widened. Irregular cascade building position on the left side of the street gives a unique impression, especially a tower building that closes the perspective of Bohdan Khmelnytsky Street and the building of 'Ukraine' hotel situated on the hill against the International Center of Culture and Arts. The cascade of fountains at the bottom of the hotel gives the impression of movement, freshness, and lightness, especially in hot summer days. A history of Khreschatyk is a history of experimental construction site. Every 15-20 years the street was undergoing major reconstructions. That is why from the architectural point of view Khreschatyk is an irregular collection of buildings and sculptures of

View of Maidan Nezalezhnosti (Independence Square)

Memorial plaque to the Prime Minister of Israel Golda Meir

The monument to the actor Mykola Yakovchenko (2000, by V. Chepelyk and others)

Memorial plaque (by V. Seliber) to the writer V. Nekrasov in Passage

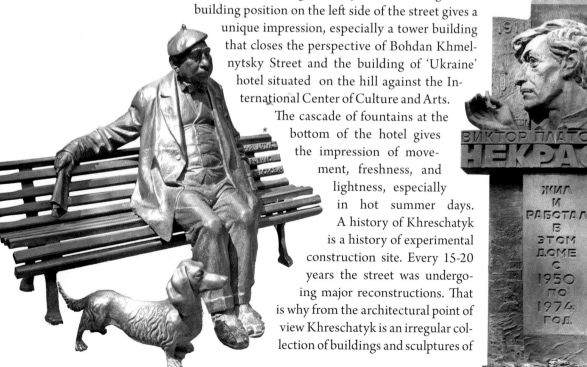

inconceivable styles. It gives the street a distinctive atmosphere of liveliness. Although Khreschatyk was built in eclectic manner, it is possible to say that this street has some special magnetism. And this might be the place to recollect words of the famous chansonnier and poet born in Kyiv, *A. Vertynsky*, 'I am willing to kiss your streets.'

Khreschatyk never falls asleep. There is a lot of night clubs, casinos and restaurants here. There is also a multi-storeyed **underground Khreschatyk** with shops and bistros.

Next to Khreschatyk the **House with Chimeras,** one of the most famous buildings that worth seeing, is situated. It was designed by Kyiv architect *Vladyslav Horodetsky*. Sculptural decorations of the building were made by an Italian sculptor *E. Sala*. From the House with Chimeras you can walk down to the **Ivan Franko National Academic Drama Theatre** (1896-1898). Horodetskoho Street (former Nikolayevskaya) leads from it to Khreschatyk. This most 'polished' street became favourite with bohemia even before the revolution. The creative union of Artists, Writers, Actors and Musicians – KhLAM (in Russian sounds similar to 'trash') was situated here, and *Les' Kurbas*, a theater reformer, started his carrier in the 'Arts Cellar' (the club of the Molody Theatre). Brilliant poets and writers *I. Erenburg, P. Tychyna, O. Mandelshtam, V. Mayakovsky* could be met in the clubs in Nikolayevskaya Street.

The flowering chestnuts on Khreshchatyk

The bird's eye view on Maidan Nezalezhnosti (Independence Square)

The monument to V. Horodetsky in Passage (2004, by V. Schur, V. Syvko)

Monument to the character of 'The Golden Calf' by Ilf and Petrov, Mikhail Panikovsky (1998, sculp. V. Schur, V. Syvko, archt. V. Skulsky)

Neptune with the nymph Amphitrite and a dolphin' bas-relief in Passage (archt. P. Andreev)

Bessarabka neighbourhood. Covered market

On Independence Square

Euro 2012 Fan-Zone on Khreschatyk before final match Spain-Italy

Independence Square is the centre of Khreschatyk and Kyiv's main square. During national holidays and celebrations the square turns into an open-air concert site where dozens of thousands of Kyivites and tourists gather to listen to their favourite singers. Military parades and demonstrations where the President of Ukraine and the members of the Government are present carried out here twice a year at Victory Day and Independence Day.

St. Alexander's Roman Catholic Cathedral built in 1817-1842 is situated in Kostyolna Street next to Independence Square.

A small alleyway goes up from Independence Square. Here one can find a little neat house where brilliant Ukrainian poet and painter *Taras Shevchenko* lived in 1846-1847. Today the **Taras Shevchenko Memorial House-Museum** is located in this building (8A Shevchenko Lane). His personal belongings and painting materials are kept here.

Yevropeiska Square is situated at the eastern end of Khreschatyk. The **National Philharmonic Society** and business and exhibition centre '**Ukrainian House**' are located there.

66

Art Nouveau and Eclecticism at the Turn of the 20ᵗʰ c.

After a regular railway communication between Kyiv and Balta had been launched in 1870, Kyiv became the biggest transport junction and the centre of the South-Western Region of the Russian Empire. The best evidence for this is the city's population growth rates: in 1865 – 71,365, in 1897 – 247,723, in 1914 — 630,000.

Kyiv turned into the biggest financial, commercial, industrial, and cultural center. The change in the status resulted into a construction boom. Up to 1000 buildings per year were built at the beginning of the 20ᵗʰ century! Kyiv nobility, not being stranger to vanity, was trying to show itself in full grandeur. Lavish decorations of houses and estates underscored this. The best architects of the empire were being invited to Kyiv, and as the nobility craved for being the most up-to-date, it promoted the latest ideas and innovations in architecture, layout, and interiors. Kyivites especially fell in love with Art Nouveau that became fashionable in Europe at the end of the 19ᵗʰ c. This should not surprise anyone. The bright aesthetics of the style, its arabesque lines, lack of abrupt motions backed with energetic asymmetry – all fitted mild, flexible, and dynamic Kyivites' character absolutely. Art Nouveau and Eclecticism became an integrated part of Kyiv's environment, reflecting the multicultural nature of the city, a crossroad of civilizations. Beautiful samples of Art Nouveau can be found in Kyiv, moreover, one can see Art Nouveau merging with all possible styles: Gothic, Empire, Renaissance, Baroque. Even the Moresque style was affected by Modern Style (**Karaite Kenesa** (Church), 7 Yaroslaviv Val, by *V. Horodetsky*, 1899-1902).

A true gem of Kyiv is sure to have been Nikolayevskaya Street, which today is named in honour of the architect *V. Horodetsky*, one of the Kyiv's most favorite architects. This part of the city is called 'Paris Corner'. Unfortunately, Soviet army blew up the luxurious 'Continentale' hotel (a conservatoire sits on this site presently) and the biggest in Europe Circus of Krutikov (a horse trainer) together with the whole Khreschatyk in 1941. The circus built in Art Nouveau had a huge hall (2000 seats) and perfect acoustics that enabled its usage for concerts. *Fyodor Shalyapin* and *Leonid Sobinov, Titto Ruffo* and *Sarah Bernhardt* performed here. Now the cinema theater 'Ukraine' stands on this site. Among the destroyed structures there was one of the largest buildings in the Russian empire – 12-storeyed 'skyscraper', known as 'Guinsburg's House'. Now the 'Ukraine' hotel is situated there. The street's pre-war luxury is still visible. Many remarkable buildings of that times remained in it, for example another house built for *Lev Guinsburg* (building **No. 9**, 1900-1906, by *G. Schleifer, E. Bradtmann*), as well as buildings **No. 11** (1895-1897, by *V. Horodetsky*), **No. 13** (1895-1897, by. *V. Horodetsky and M. Klug*), **No. 15** (Art Nouveau, 1900-1901, by *E. Bradtman* and *G. Schleifer*) and **No.17/1** (1909, Northern Modern style, by *I. Belyaev*).

The **Passage**, which was designed by architect *P. Andreyev* in Classicist Modern style in 1913-1915, runs parallel to Horodetskoho Street. The arch entrance was added in 1950 (by *A. Vlasov* and *A. Dobrovolsky*). It permanently keeps the pre-revolutionary spirit of cosy coffee-houses and refined boutiques. A number of initial pre-revolutionary buildings attract attention on **Khreschatyk**. They used

Building No. 39 in Volodymyrska Str. (archt. K. Schimann, 1900-1901). This is here where the famous confectioner's shop 'Marquise' menioned by M. Bulgakov in 'The White Guard' was located

The fragment of the 'House with Cats' façade (23 Hoholivska Str., 1909, archt. V. Bessmertny)

St. Maria's Commune of Red Cross Nurses house (75 Saksahanskoho Str., archt. V. Rykov, sculptor F. Balavensky, 1913)

The part of the building at
11 Horodetskoho Str.
(1895-1897, by V. Horodetsky)

The fragment of
L. Rodzianko's house
(14 Yaroslaviv Val Str.,
1910-1911, by M. Klug)

The fragment of
L. Rodzianko's house
(14B Yaroslaviv
Val Str., 1908-1911,
by M. Yaskevych)

The House with
Chimeras (1901-1902,
archt. V. Horodetsky,
sculp. E. Sala)

to house banks (**No. 8**, Petersburg Bank, 1911-1914, by *L. Benoua*; **No. 10**, Volzhsko-Kamsky Bank, 1912-1913, by *P. Andreyev*; **No. 32**, Foreign Commerce Bank, 1913-1915, by *F. Lidval*).

There were numerous hotels in Kyiv before the revolution. Among the preserved ones are: the oldest **Canet's hotel** (40 Khreschatyk Street, 1873-1874, by *V. Nikolayev*; the painter *M. Vrubel* lived there in 1888-1889), **hotels 'Palais-Royal'** (rebuilt), **'Berlin'**, **'National'** in Bessarabka neighbourhood, and a bit upwards Taras Shevchenko Boulevard, Art Nouveau buildings of hotels 'Palace' and 'Marceille' (today **Premier Palace Hotel**). The area was dominated with a magnificent building of the covered Bessarabsky **market built** in Modern Style in 1912 (by *G. Hai*).

Velyka Vasylkivska Street starts at Bessarabska Square. It looks as if it were a part of Khreschatyk. Many more pre-revolutionary buildings have been preserved there, including the most attractive buildings **No. 14** (Northern Modern Style, 1914), and No. 18 (**small passage** with Art Nouveau elements).

In addition to the center, the whole city is dotted with a true constellation of outstanding late 19th – early 20th cc. architecture samples. Among the interesting areas are **Lypky** in Pechersk, Yaroslaviv Val, Velyka Zhytomyrska, Honchara, Volodymyrska, Kostyolna, Reitarska, Saksahanskoho Streets; Muzeiny Lane; Kontraktova Square.

Kyivites are fond of giving nicknames to the most favourite and astonishing houses. There are such examples of this: **'the House with Chimeras'** (10 Bankova Street), **'the House of Weeping Widow'** (23 Luteranska Street), **'the House with Caryatids'** (3 Pylypa Orlyka Street), **'the House with Snakes'** (32 Velyka Zhytomyrska Street), **'the House with Cats'** or **'the House with Owls'** (23 Hoholivska Street), **'the Chocolate House'** (17 Shovkovychna Street), **'the Museum with Lions'** (6 Hrushevskoho Street). They are surrounded with legends and striking stories. The best houses have preserved interiors' decoration fragments, the most interesting one being the theater's premises in Art Nouveau at 14B Yaroslaviv Val Street.

Stained-glass window in the 'Suziria' Theater

The mansion of baron M. L. Steingel (1 Yaroslaviv Val Str., 1896-1898, archt. M. Dobachevsky)

Former municipal school of the professor M. Bunge (5/18 Pylyp Orlyk Str., archts. G. Schleifer and E. Bradtmann)

1, 2. Fragments of the 'House with Cats' façade (23 Hoholivska Str., 1909, archt. V. Bessmertny)

3. Atlantes on the façade of the building No. 7 in Kostyolna Street (1910, archt. I. Ledukhovsky, sculp. F. Sokolov)

4. 'The House of Weeping Widow' (23 Luteranska Str., 1907, by E. Bradtmann). You can find the traces of tears under the woman's eyes rain or shine

5. Chimeras on the façade of baron M. L. Steingel's mansion (1 Yaroslaviv Val Str.)

6. The façade of the former profit-making house at 5 Shevchenko Blvd. (1908, archts. E. Bradtmann and M. Drobotun)

7. Ginzburg's House (1900-1906, archts. G. Schleifer and E. Bradtmann)

8. The mansion of baron Uxkull-Gyllenband (19 Shovkovychna Str., 1901, archt. M. Vyshnevsky)

9. Former Karaite Kenesa (7 Yaroslaviv Val Str., 1902, archt. V. Horodetsky, sculp. E. Sala)

8

9

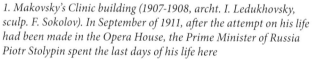

1. *Makovsky's Clinic building (1907-1908, archt. I. Ledukhovsky, sculp. F. Sokolov). In September of 1911, after the attempt on his life had been made in the Opera House, the Prime Minister of Russia Piotr Stolypin spent the last days of his life here*

2. *Former clergy house (1912, archt. V. Eisner)*

3. *Passage (1913-1915, archt. P. Andreyev). From the Khreschatyk side Passage begins with the arch decorated with the Soviet symbols (1951, archts. A. Vlasov, A. Dobrovolsky, B. Pryimak)*

4. *The statue of Phryne, a Greek hetaera who became a model for the sculptor Praxiteles. Mogilevtsev's house (4 Museiny Lane, sculp. F. Balavensky)*

5. *Building No. 31/16 in Reitarska Street (archt. M. Yaskevych)*

6. *The part of Ginsburg's house at 9 Horodetskoho Str.*

7. *Art Nouveau paintings of the ceiling in the 'Suzirya' Theater foyer*

8. *Building No. 99 in Saksahanskoho Street (1911-1912)*

9. *The part of the former 8th Gymnasium building (5 Franka Sq., 1899, Eclecticism, by M. Dobachevsky). The future 'God of Dance' Serge Lifar studied there*

Kyiv Pechersk Lavra

On pages 74-75: Bird's eye view on Lavra and the Dnieper

Kyiv-Pechersk Lavra and monastery buildings as viewed from the south

The main entrance to Lavra – the Holy Gates

On pages 78-79: Lavra in winter

In 1051 Rus monk *Anthony* came back from the Mount Athos with the blessing of the Holy Mountain. After long wanderings he settled in a small secluded cave dug out by *Hilarion* who later became the metropolitan of Kyiv. Other monks started settling around him, so the monastery and the **Far Caves of Lavra** appeared. In 1062 St. Anthony, who liked solitude, left the monastery, dug out a cave at the bottom of the nearby hill and founded **Near Caves** where he lived and was buried in 1071. Monks elected *St. Theodosy* to be the Father Superior of the monastery. St. Theodosy adopted a strict monastic rule of Greek Studite Monastery known as 'Studite Charter' that he received from the Studite monk who had came to Kyiv with the suite of the new Greek metropolitan George. Later on this rule was adopted by all the monasteries of Kyivan Rus and St. Theodosy was called the founder of monasticism in Russia. Since then Pechersk Monastery has became a prototype for Rus' monasteries.

Some of monastery's ascetics chose the life of hermits. They used to dig out small caves and prayed there for the salvation of the world without leaving them for many years. In these caves their souls were leaving their bodies. Their Holy Relics stay incorruptible to our days. The **Holy Relics of Christian Saints** are healing, and the heads of some of the ascetics exhale the chrism. Modern science is not able to explain this phenomenon.

The relics of *St. Anthony, St. Alypius, St. Agapit, St. Damian, St. Nestor the Chronicler*, and epic hero *Elijah of Murom* are buried in the Caves of Lavra. Up to now 122 relics of ascetics remain in the caves. This is the reason why Kyiv is also called a Holy City.

The caves of Kyiv are special sacral areas. There are more than 45 caves in Kyiv, beginning with the famous Lavra caves, after which the monastery Kyiv-Pechersk Lavra was called, and ending with less investigated **Zverinets** caves, **Kyrylivski** caves, caves under **St. Sophia's Cathedral**, in **Holy Trinity Monastery** in **Kytayiv**, caves next to **Askoldova Mohyla** ('the grave of Askold'), and many others.

In 1073 the Father Superior *St. Theodosy* and the bishop *Michael* laid a cathedral in honour of the Mother of God. According to the legend, Byzantium stonemasons saw the cathedral in a cloud and came

His Beatitude Volodymyr Metropolitan of Kyiv and all Ukraine holds a moleben (thanksgiving service) on the feast of The Entry of Our Lord into Jerusalem (Palm Sunday) in the refectory church of Kyiv-Pechersk Lavra

The Divine Liturgy is celebrated at the Church of the Exaltation of the Holy Cross in the Far Caves of Kyiv-Pechersk Lavra

The interior of Dormition Cathedral of Lavra

The Church of All Saints (1696-1698) over the Economic gates and monastery cells. On the background, the Church of Our Saviour at Berestovo (1113-1125)

On pages 82-83: The view on the right bank of the Dnieper and on Lavra from Hydropark at sunset

Fortress wall around the Far and the Near Caves. Church in honour of the Icon of the Mother of God 'The Life-Bearing Spring'

The Church of Our Saviour at Berestovo (1113 – 1125)

to Kyiv to build it. They were told by the Mother of God to bring an icon of the Dormition that she gave them to Kyiv. That is why the temple was named a **Dormition Cathedral**. The cathedral was built at the sight that was marked by nature – it remained dry at night dew. It became the centre of Upper Lavra – the part of the monastery that was built above the ground. For centuries Kyiv and Lithuanian princes and high clergy were being buried in the cathedral. There was a grave of princess *Uliana of Tver* (died in 1392) who became the wife of Lithuanian prince *Algirdas* and the mother of Polish king *Jogaila*. Kyiv princes of Lithuanian period – descendants of *Algirdas* and *Olelko*, the *Ostrozhskys* and the *Vyshnevetskys* were also intered here. There were also graves of the scientist and poet *P. Berynda* (died in 1632), Metropolitan *P. Mohyla* (died in 1646), Kyiv Archimandrite *I. Giesel* (died in 1683).

The monastery was becoming more and more famous, and in 1159 *Andrey Bogolubsky*, the son of prince *Yuri Dolgorukiy*, gave the monastery the title of 'Lavra' and the status of stavropegion that put it in the direct subordination to Patriarch. 'Lavra' is a Greek word that means 'a street' or 'a village'. This title was given to the biggest and the most respected monasteries. By this time Kyiv-Pechersk Lavra became the stronghold of Christianity and the major centre of the enlightenment and cultural life.

The writing of Russian chronicles originates from Lavra. In 1113 the *chronicler St. Nestor* finished his renowned old Slavic chronicle, 'The Story of the Passing Years' here.

Lavra was also the centre for the development of medicine in Kyivan Rus. *St. Agapit*, *St. Damian*, and *St. Peter of Syria* were the famous monastic healers. In the 12th c. prince *Sviatoslav* (known as *Nikolai Sviatosha*) founded the first hospital in Kyiv here.

Lavra was well known for its icon-painting school that was headed by *St. Alypius* and *St. Gregory*.

In 1615 a **printing house** was founded in the monastery. In 1627 the first dictionary of the Church Slavonic language 'Lexicon' and in 1674 the first book on

the history of Ukraine called 'Synopsis' (by *Innozenz Giesel*) were published here. The books contained marvellous engravings and miniatures. You may familiarise yourself with the production of old monastic printing-house in the **Museum of Book and Book Printing** that is situated at the territory of Lavra.

Dormition Cathedral and the Church of St. Anthony and St. Theodosius

Nowadays Lavra is a unique architectural ensemble that was included in the UNESCO World Heritage List. Holiness and divine beauty of this place leaves a feeling of unity with God. This feeling is intensified by the monastery's position on the picturesque Pechersk hills. There are many viewers lookout sites here, which provide a magnificent view of Lavra shrines and the left bank of the Dnieper river.

The cupolas of Lavra are gold plated. According to church symbolism, golden colour symbolises golden sunrays and the Holy Spirit. Cupolas are also often painted green. In this case green colour symbolises life, spring and renovation, it consists of two colours: blue – a symbol of the Holy Spirit, and yellow – a symbol of God the Son. The golden cupolas signify 'the edge of the sun appearing above the horizon'. In the fair weather golden cupola of the **Great Lavra Belfry** (1745) that is 96,5 m high was seen from dozens kilometres away. Its shine was the guiding star for many pilgrims who were coming to Lavra to pray to the Saints and to be cleansed from their sins.

The monument to the hospodar (prince) of Moldavia Constantine Ypsilanti (1818, 1997)

The total area of Lavra ensemble is 24 hectares. You can find 122 architectural monuments of the 11th-20th cc. and 14 churches (including 6 cave churches) here.

The total length of the caves is more than 1,000 meters. There are two **ancient wells** there that, according to the legend, were dug by *St. Anthony* and *St. Theodosy*. A church in honour of the Icon of the Mother of God 'The Life-Bearing Spring' was erected next to the wells.

The Church of the Saviour at Berestovo is worth mentioning as well. The founder of Moscow, prince *Yuriy Dolgorukiy*, is buried in this church. The frescos in the church are dated to the 12th c. There one can find a unique fresco called 'Miraculous Fishing' pained on one of the walls. The size of this fresco is 100 sq. m.

Nowadays Lavra houses a lot of museums at its territory. It is worth mentioning that Lavra was repeatedly robbed during its long history. The Bolsheviks in 1920s and the fascists during World War II destroyed a great number of invaluable Orthodox sacred objects. Some of them were sold abroad in 1930s. Thus in Los-Angeles Museum of Arts (USA) you can find silver gold-plated Holy Gates from the **Church of the Nativity of the Most-Holy Mother of God** (1784) and from the **Church of Exaltation of the Holy Cross** (1767).

An Orthodox monastery, Kyiv Theological Seminary, and Academy are also situated at the territory of Lower Lavra.

Churches and Monasteries

St. Panteleimon's Cathedral in Feofania (1905-1912)

St. Nicolas' Jordan Church, which stands at the spot where St. Nicolas' Jordan Monastery founded in 1616 used to stand

Kyiv-Pechersk Lavra is one of the major monasteries in the Orthodox world, but there are many others in Kyiv. Spirituality in Rus has been reflected by number of monasteries ('monk' from the Greek – solitary). The monasteries influenced greatly both the spiritual life of the church and the laity.

Among the most ancient monasteries is **Vydubytsky Monastery**. It is mentioned for the first time in 1070. It is here where Prince Volodymyr threw the wooden statue for the heathen god Perun into the Dnieper during the christening of Rus in 988. The architectural ensemble was completed in the 17th-18th cc. The oldest **St. Michael's Cathedral** was built in 1076. The magnificent Ukrainian baroque **St. George's Cathedral** was built between 1696 and 1701 on funds donated by the Starodub colonel *M. Miklashevsky*. The cartouche with his coat-of-arms has been preserved in the **Refectory Church of the Saviour**. The four-tier bell tower (1727-1733) was built on funds donated by Hetman *Danylo Apostol*. The famous pedagogue *K. Ushynsky*, founders of the Kyiv Art Museum *B.* and *V. Khanenkos*, the professor of anatomy *V. Bets* are buried on the monastery's territory.

St. Michael's Golden-Domed Monastery was founded in 1108 by Great Prince *Svyatopolk Izyaslavych* (christened Michael). **St. Michael's Golden-Domed Cathedral** is dedicated to Archangel Michael, the heaven protector of Kyiv. In 1108 Princess Barbara, a daughter of Byzantine Emperor Alexios Komnenos and a spouse of Great Prince Svyatopolk Izyaslavych, before going to Kyivan Rus, asked her father to present her with the healing relics of Great Martyr Barbara (Saint Barbara). Kept initially in St. Michael's Cathedral, now they are in St. Volodymyr's Cathedral.

In 1936, St. Michael's Cathedral was blown up, and the unique frescoes and mosaics taken from its walls are kept today in St. Sophia's Cathedral in Kyiv ('The Eucharist', 'St. Stephen and St. Thaddaeus', 'Annunciation', ornaments), in the

Russian Museum in Saint-Petersburg, and in the Tretiakov Gallery in Moscow (a magnificent mosaic 'St. Demetrius of Thessalonica'). The cathedral was rebuilt in 1996-2000 in Ukrainian Baroque style it received in the 18th c. after the reconstruction by *I. Hryhorovych-Barsky*. The **refectory with the Church of St. John the Theologian** (1713, Ukrainian baroque) has preserved in the monastery's territory. Splendid views of St. Sophia Cathedral and the Dnieper open from the monastery belltower.

The founder of **Holy Trinity Monastery** in Zvirynets–*Iona of Kyiv*–had a gift for healing. The oldest clock in Kyiv manufactured in Paris in 1858 can be found in the monastery. It is also famous for the **Zvirynetski caves** where underground churches existed in the ancient times.

The other **Holy Trinity Monastery** in Kytayiv is located in an especially scenic site. According to the legend, the monastery excisted in 1151. In the 18th c. this monastery was glorified by *Rev. Dosifey* who stayed there and was famous for his astuteness. Empress *Elisabeth*, Peter's daughter, spoke with him in 1744. Dosifey blessed *Seraphim* (*P. Moshnin*, the future hermit *Seraphim Sarovsky*) before he went to Sarov Monastery (Russia). **Holy Trinity Cathedral** (1783-1767, Ukrainian baroque), the **Church of the Saint Twelve Apostles** (1835) and **St. Seraphim Sarovsky's Church** have been preserved in the monastery. Kytay hill still hides ancient **monk caves**. The monastery's location in the brooks bend and surrounded with ponds offers peaceful harmony to any visitor.

The Monastery of the Presentation of the Mother of God (founded in 1878) in Pechersk is famous for the icon of the Mother of God 'Care for humility'. In 1993 the icon transferred its own negative imprint on the icon stand glass that had not been even touched. Numerous scientific investigations did not manage to explain this phenomenon. Ever since the image and its imprint have acquired healing properties.

Metropolitan *Petro Mohyla* founded **Holy Intercession Monastery** in Holosiyiv in 1631. Later it became a summer residence of Kyiv metropolitans.

St. Panteleimon's Convent in Feofania was established in 1901 as a cloister in honor of *St. Innokentiy (Borisov)*. He was here in 1836-1841 and named all ponds, bridges and springs of Feofania

Holy Intercession Monastery in Holosiyiv

M. Hryshko National Botanical Garden. Holy Trinity Cathedral of Holy Trinity Iona Monastery

*St. Nicolas'
Cathedral (1911) of
Holy Intercession
Monastery and its
interior*

after names mentioned in the Gospel. Hence the name **Iosaphat Valley** comes from. As for the name 'Feofania', it originates from the name of Chyhyryn Bishop and at the same time the Father Superior of St. Michael's Golden-Domed Monastery *Feofan (Shyianov)* who was granted this land as country residence for Chyhyryn bishops in 1800. There are a lot of curative springs within the monastery, among them St. Panteleimon's one is the most famous.

The complex of **St. Flor's Convent** had formed during the 17th-19th cc. The most remarkable buildings are the **Church of Ascension** (1722-1732), the **Church of St. Nickolas of Myra in Lycia** (the first tier – the 17th c., the second one – 1818), the rotunda **Church of Resurrection** (1824, classicism, by *A. Melensky*), and the **bell-tower** (1732-1821).

Intercession Convent was founded in 1889 by Great Princess *Alexandra Petrovna* (died in 1900), nèe Princess de Auldenburg. She donated all her money for its beautification. Other members of imperial family helped her as well. Here she took monastic vows under the name of *Anastasia*. The whole system of charity institutions – a hospital for women, a school for girls, orphanages and asylums for poor children of all social classes, for incurable women–was created at the convent. The best Kyiv doctors worked here. **St. Nickolas' Cathedral** with 6 altars is the biggest in Kyiv. The cathedral was built in 1896-1911 according to draft design by the son of Great Princess *Peter Romanov* and working plans by the architect *V. Nikolayev*. The capacity is up to 3000 people.

The architectural ensemble of **Bratsky Monastery** (17th-19th cc.) is also of interest. Now Kyiv-Mohyla Academy occupies its territory.

St. Cyril's Church was built in 1146 and was used as a family burial vault of Princes *Olgovychs* of Chernihiv. Prince *Svyatoslav Vsevolodovych*, one of the heroes of the epic 'The Lay of the Host of Igor', was buried in this church in 1194. Here you can see 800 sq. m of the 12th- century frescos and majestic wall paintings by *M. Vrubel* including a famous 'The Mother of God with a Baby'. Nowadays a museum is located here.

St. Volodymyr's Cathedral was built to commemorate the 900th anniversary of the Baptism of Rus, designed in Byzantine style by architects *I. Stromm, P. Sparro,* and *A. Beretti*. It is enormous in size and famous for interior painting made by Russian artists *V. Vasnetsov, M. Nesterov, M. Vrubel,* Ukrainian painters *V. Zamyrailo, S. Kostenko, M. Pymonenko,* and Polish painters *P. Svedomsky* and *W. Kotarbinski* under the supervision of professor *A. Prakhov*. The mosaics of the interior of the cathedral were made by Venetian masters. The main entrance door was designed by *A. Prakhov.*

Kyiv has always been an Orthodox city. Nevertheless from ancient times it has been tolerant to all world religions. That is why Kyiv is sometimes called 'Northern Jerusalem'. Apart from a great number of Orthodox churches you can find here many other houses of worship, churches and cathedrals where those who practice other religions come to pray.

You can visit majestic Kyiv **synagogues**. Jews has been living in Kyiv since ancient times. The first references to Jews living in the city are dated to the 10th c. Since then synagogues have always existed here. The oldest remained synagogue built in Moresque style in 1895 can be found in Podil district in Schekavytska Street. **Kyiv chorus synagogue**, which was founded in 1898 and built in the untypical for such type of buildings pseudo-Moresque style, is situated at 13 Shota Rustaveli Street.

Muslim Centre and the mosque **"Ar Rahma" (Mercy)** were built at Schekavytsa hill in Lukianivska Str. There is also another mosque at **Islamic Cultural Centre** in Dehtyarivska Street.

The oldest synagogue in Kyiv (1895)

Lutheran Church (1857)

The mosque at Schekavytsya hill

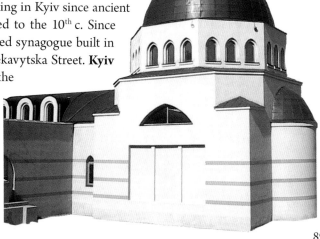

*St. Volodymyr's
Cathedral
(1862-1882)
and its interior*

*Tserkovschyna
(Khutir Vilnyi).
St. Nicolas'
Church (19th c.)*

The fragment of St. Nicolas' Roman Catholic Cathedral decoration. In the centre there is a sculpture of Archangel Michael

The Interior of St. Nicolas' Roman Catholic Cathedal

The visit of the Pope John Paul II to Kyiv

St. Nicolas' Roman Catholic Cathedal (1899-1909, archt. V. Horodetsky)

On pages 94-95: The view on Vydubytsky Monastery from M. Hryshko National Botanical Garden

Lutheran church built in 1855-1857 can be found in Luteranska Street. German Evangelist and Lutheran Community of Kyiv hold services here. Next to the church there was a settlement of German community – descendants of colonists invited to Kyiv by *Catherine the Great*. The church was named after Saint Catherine who was the patron saint of the Russian Empress.

At **St. Alexander's Roman Catholic Cathedral** services are held in Ukrainian, Russian, Polish, French, and English. There is also another beautiful **Roman Catholic cathedral** in Kyiv named after **St. Nicolas** that was built in 1899-1909 by *V. Horodetsky*. The height of the cathedral is 60 meters. Its sculptural decorations were made by an Italian sculptor *E. Sala*. The cathedral has a wonderful organ; services and concerts are held here. On the left bank of the Dnieper river in Voskresenka district a Roman Catholic Centre was constructed. And the **Resurrection Greek Catholic Cathedral** was built near Livoberezhna underground station in 2011.

There are also houses of worship of Protestant communities in Kyiv.

Parks

When you enter the parks of Kyiv, you will realize why Kyiv is called the garden city. There are so many parks in Kyiv that even without trying you can find a quiet little corner or a solitary bench. Kyivan benches are a special part of the city's life. They are found everywhere, even in the most secluded places. How many dramatic stories would be revealed to us if they could only talk! How many declarations of love! And how many broken hearts were left shattered at their pedestals. But life in Kyiv never stops, not even for a second. Kyiv was created for love, and Kyivan parks celebrate this.

For each Kyivite there are around a 1,000 sq. m of greenery. The city has about 70 parks, many of which have reservoirs. Kyivan parks gracefully blend into forest areas and meadow park zones. As a whole, the green zone occupies 383,000 hectares. Within the city, an area of 40 sq. km is covered by water, among which are picturesque verdant islands and parks. This combination of hills, greenery and water give Kyiv its unique charm.

The first park in Kyiv was laid out by Metropolitan *P. Mohyla* in 1631 in the metropolitan courtyard in **Holosiyiv**. Several unique **oak trees** as old as 1,000 years are still standing there. The **National ExpoCenter of Ukraine** is situated in Holosiyiv. And near it, in Pyrohiv, there is an open-air **Museum of Folk Architecture and Everyday Life in Ukraine** (http://pirogovo.org.ua). Here, covering an area of 150 hectares, in the midst of a scenic landscape more than 300 objects of folk wooden architecture as well as a collection of 80,000 items of everyday life can be found. All historic-ethnocultural regions of Ukraine are represented here. Some of the cottages and churches date back to the 16th-18th cc. They were carefully removed from various regions in Ukraine and placed in a natural environment maximizing its approximation to the original setting.

The most beloved and visited parks are the terraces along the banks of the Dnieper. Among them is **Volodymyrska hill**, where the **monument to Prince Volodymyr** (1853) is situated. In the year of 988, intent on strengthening his regional power, Volodymyr introduced Christianity as the official religion of the realm.

In the 1740s, **Tsar's Garden** (now known as City Garden) was laid out according to B. Rastrelli's design. Here there is **Mariinsky Palace** (1750-1755) named in honour of *Maria*, the wife of Tsar *Alexander II*. Today the palace is used for official ceremonies and is closed to the public. Next to it there is **Verkhovna Rada** (Ukrainian Parliament) **building** and the viewers lookout, which has a clear view of **Metro Bridge** and the left bank.

Another unique park is **M. Hryshko National Botanical Garden** located in the historical area of **Zvirynets** and **Vydubychi**. Its huge 130hectare area is saturated with the richest collection of plants, many of which are rare species. The collection encompasses 13,000 different types and varieties. Such botanical geographic landscapes as 'The Crimea', 'The Caucasus', 'The Far East', and 'The Carpathians' are represented here. In he park there is a unique collection of orchids. In addition, the orchid 'Dorotis the Beautiful', which was breeded by local selectionists, in 1980 grew and flowered in an outer space capsule. A greenhouse has an area

Holy Trinity Cathedral (1763-1767) of Holy Trinity Monastery in Kytayiv

The best place for a rest – benches under the chestnut trees

Australian palm tree of 200 years old in A. Fomin Botanical Garden

The descent to the
monument of Magdeburg
rights

Mass bathing on Epiphany
(the 19th of January) in
Hydropark

The Church of
St. Parasceva the Friday
(18th c.) in the Museum
of Folk Architecture and
Everyday Life in Ukraine

Windmills in Pyrohiv

Pyrohiv in winter

of 8 thousand sq m. It houses expositions of cactuses and other succulents, tropical fruit plants, 700 species of orchids, 60 species of azaleas, and delightful camellias.

Here you can see an unforgettable spectacle: the blossoming of deciduous magnolias with huge white, pink, and red fragrant flowers. The effect is magnified when one hears the pealing of the bells of **Holy Trinity Iona Monastery**, which is located on slightly higher ground.

The special energy of this place has a beneficial effect on the bountiful lilac garden – the pride of National Botanical Garden. All the blossoming lilac hues from intense violet to blinding white flow in waves and stream down to Vydubytsky Monastery (11th-18th cc.).

These surprising and inimitable landscapes attracted and inspired painters at all the times to create thousands of paintings. And you become so inspired, enjoying the view of sparkling golden and sapphire domes of St. Michael's (11th c.) and St. George's Cathedrals (1686-1701) on the background of blossoming lilacs.

In **A. Fomin Botanical Garden** next to Taras Shevchenko University you will also find a special collection of plants. The garden was planted in 1839. The oldest in Ukraine Australian palm tree (200 years old) and araucaria bidwillii (150 years old) grow here in a 30-meter-high climate controlled greenhouse together with the collection of rare epiobiotic plants. In whole, the botanical gardens number 10,000 species and forms of plants.

In **Pechersk Landscape Park** there is a **National Museum of the History of the Great Patriotic War**. Opened in 1981, this memorial complex occupies an area of 10 hectares and incorporates a museum (18 galleries), an eternal flame, plaques honouring hero cities, and a display ground for World War II vintage and more recent military equipment. Seven compositions comprising 100 bronze sculptures lining the road to the complex are good examples of traditional Soviet style sculpture with their powerful portrayal of human strength. The sculptures symbolize the heroic struggle against the fascists. The centre of the composition of the complex is a gigantic titanium alloy female figure with a sword and shield in her hands intended to symbolize the Soviet 'Motherland' –

Mariinsky Palace, a government residence

Pechersk Landscape Park. The exhibition of tulips

The composition from the flower exhibition in Pechersk Landscape Park. The dove of peace above the outline of Ukraine

On pages 102-103:

Bessarabka at night

Multifunctional complex 'Gulliver'

Light and music fountains on Poshtova Square

Magnolias in blossom near Holy Trinity Iona Monastery in M. Hryshko National Botanical Garden

Mountain Garden Section in M. Hryshko Botanical Garden

A pond in M. Rylsky Holosiyivsky Park

On pages 106-107: **Hydropark** *is a park on the island on the Dnieper in the Kyiv's center, the favourite recreational place for inhabitants of Kyiv*

Small pedestrian bridge

The view on Metro Bridge and Kyiv-Pechersk Lavra from the beach

At botton: The European Wakeboard Masters contest on Venetian Channel. On the background there is an exposition complex and Resurrection Greek Catholic Cathedral

'the Rodina Mat'. 62-meter-high monument was designed by *V. Borodai, V. Yelizarov*, and others. The height of the sculpture together with the pedestal is 102 meters, and the entire monument weighs 530 tons. Not only the size of the monument but also its details are noteworthy. For example, the sword alone is 16 meters in length and weighs 12 tons. The museum's exhibits consist of 8,000 objects reflecting various stages and aspects of World War II. Every year at the Independence Day a magic festival – **Flower Exhibition** takes place in the park at the territory of the museum.

A **Zoo** that was founded in 1908 is a worth visiting site of Kyiv. On the territory of 34 hectares you can find picturesque ponds and lakes, more than 130 species of trees and bushes. Open-air cages and pavilions for birds and animals naturally blend with this beautiful scenery. Lions, tigers, bears, and other animals live in natural environment at 'The Island of Animals'. Pavilions for exotic birds and reptiles are among the largest in Europe. More than 2,000 animals and 330 species of animals and birds live in Kyiv Zoo.

In the summertime, when the sun warms the city streets with heat rising up to 40 degrees Celsius, hundreds of thousands of Kyivites make their way to the beaches on the islands of the Dnieper or hide by the cooling lakes, which are so numerous in Kyiv.

But even here you have a choice – with difficulty you can find a free patch of sand among the dark bronzed bodies, or search for a solitary little spot on the nudist or secluded beaches and sunbathe by the water in complete isolation, and then remember with astonishment that just now you made your way with great effort through the hive. The most popular beaches – those with full service and those that are free as well as resting places – are found at the **Hydropark**. The beach volleyball and fooball world championships were held here. Summer life is a 24-hour event. Open cafes and cosy summer restaurants stretch one after the other and occupy a huge area. Many of them are open 24 hours.

Music for all tastes sounds ceaselessly, fireworks flash fleetingly, and if you get tired of the noise of the discotheques, you can take a stroll alongside the channels of the Dnieper. From the little bridge which crosses the Venetian channel you can admire the right bank of the city and the spotlight illuminated bell towers of Lavra Monastery, or complete your night time stroll with a boat ride along the Dnieper.

This unity of a large city with its luxuriant nature is the key to the phenomenon called Kyiv.

*Galleon landing stage.
Mezhyhirya*

*Honka Palace.
Mezhyhirya*

Autumn in Mezhyhirya

KIEV FASHION PARK, initiated by *Oleksandr Sokolovsky*, gained extraordinary popularity. Within this project framework, unique designer art objects – statues, installations, benches, and various small architectural forms – are installed in Kyiv parks and public gardens. The project implementation started at **Peizazhna Aleya** (Scenery Walkway) where children's park was equipped by *Konstantin Skritutskyi*'s original mosaic sculptures. There were installed fountains, sculptures of Little Prince, Zebras in Love, 30-meter-high cat-centipede, benches in the shape of rabbit, cat and crow. Then other benches, sculptures and art installations by famous Kyiv designers appeared at **Peizazhna Aleya**. This project is constantly updated with new art objects. The impression is enhanced by a magnificent panorama of Kyiv mountains, Podil and Zadneprovye.

As a result of the Revolution of Dignity, Kyivans got one more remarkable object – a nationalized luxurious residence of the escaped president *V. Yanukovich* – **Mezhyhirya**. Here, from the XII century, was founded the Mezhyhirya Savior-Transfiguration Monastery – one of the religious centers of Zaporozhian Cossacks. At the end of XVIII century the monastery was abolished, and on its territory was founded the famous Mezhyhirya Faience Factory by German Kranich, which closed in 1884. In 1933, the monastery territory (140 ha) was chosen

Kiev Fashion Park. Arch 'Rainbow'
(2011, by Aleksandr Alekseev)

Peizazhna Aleya. Bench 'Hands'
(2011, by Liliya Litkovska)

Peizazhna Aleya.
Children's Park by K. Skritutskyi

as the site of the government residence of the USSR, which later was illegally privatized by *Yanukovich*. He built a number of luxurious objects here – HONKA Palace, Galleon landing stage, a sports complex, a golf club, a yacht club, a garage with a car collection, a zoo. However, the main sight is a huge park with artificial lakes, fountains and bridges.

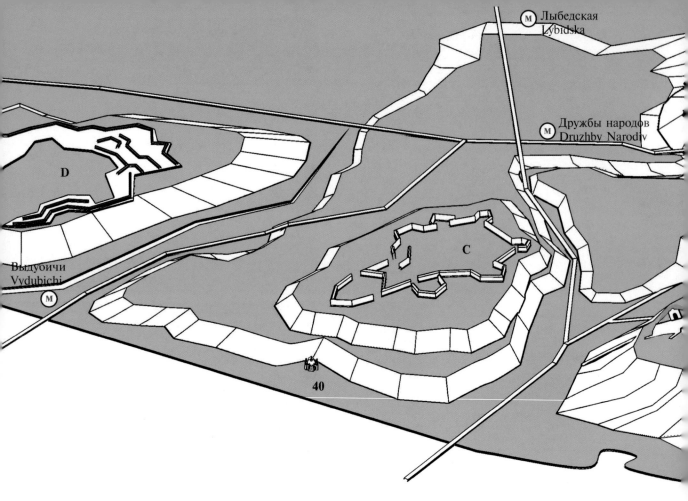

Лыбедская
Lybidska

Дружбы народов
Druzhby Narodiv

D

Выдубичи
Vydubichi

C

40

The Scheme of Pechersk Fortress

On page 114-115: Spassky bastion of Pechersk Fortress protects the Church of Our Saviour at Berestovo and Lavra. On the foreground there is an esplanade

Kyiv Fortress

Since the oldest times Kyiv has been well known as the most important strategic point in Eastern Europe. At the turn of the 11[th]c. Prince *Volodymyr* created a system of three line fortifications at the approaches to Kyiv. The far approaches were protected by 400-kilometre-long **Zmiyiv (Snake) ramparts** that impress even today. The second line stretched along the rivers Irpin, Stuhna, and Sula. It was composed of ramparts and fortresses. The third line was formed by fortified settlements around Kyiv: Bilychi, Zhuliany, Hostomel, Borky, Vyshhorod. There was a mighty fortress in Peresichen. The Turkic word for 'fortress' is 'kitay', hence the later name of this area – Kytayiv–originated. Its fortification system included three lines of ramparts and ditches partly preserved till our days. Nowadays it is a scenic territory in the south of Kyiv.

The fortification structures of Kyivan Rus have been considered above. Only the name of the hill – Zamkova (i.e. Castle) – where a well fortified castle with a pine tree log wall topped with 15 towers used to be located as well as a quite questionable reconstruction of **Pechersk gate** of Old Kyiv Fortress at Independence Square remind about the 14th-18th cc. The Cossacks burned down the castle in 1651.

Many street names indicate that Kyiv was fortress-city: Reitarska (Riders'), Striletska (Infantrymen's), Tsytadelna (Citadel), Bastionna (Bastion), Yaroslaviv Val (Yaroslav's Rampart), etc. In 1654, following the political alliance between Ukraine and Russia, Kyiv became a key frontier city at three states junction: Rzecz Pospolita (Polish-Lithuanian Commonwealth), the Osman and the Russian Empires. Starokyivska (Old Kyiv) Fortress in the Upper Town was rehabilitated. Later a decision was made to construct a fortress around Kyiv-Pechersk Lavra. In 1679 an earth fortress with 'rolls-out'–places for cannons – was started by Hetman *Samoilovych* and and General Patrick Gordon. In 1698-1701 Hetman *Mazepa* erected 5 strong towers and stone walls on the remains of the 12th-century Lavra defensive walls. The walls were 1.290 m long, 2.5-3 m

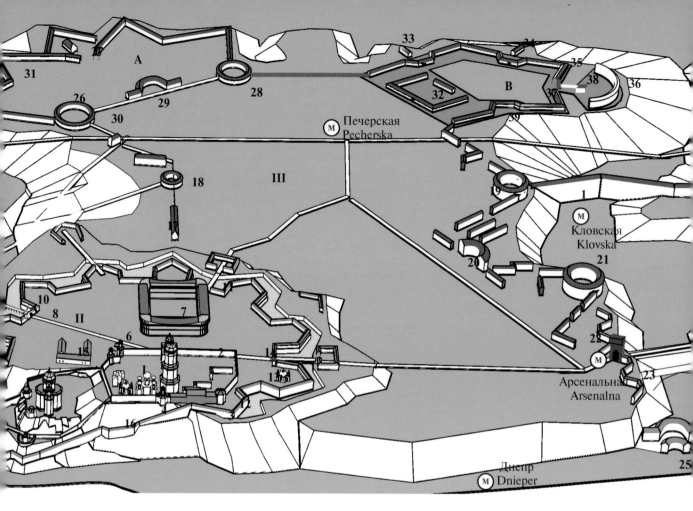

I Citadel – Lavra

1. Retrenchment – an earth rampart and a ditch
connecting Kyiv-Pechersk and Starokyivska Fortresses (17th –
early 18th cc.). Prorizna Street was laid at its place

2. Mazepa fortress walls (early 18th c.)

3. North (Malyarna) tower (1698-1701)

4. St. Onuphry's (Chamber) tower (1698-1701)

5. Southern (Horlogium) tower (1698-1701)

6. Ivan Kuschnyk's tower (1698-1701)

II Old Pechersk Fortress – Kyiv-Pechersk Citadel

7. The building of Arsenal (1784-1798)

8. Upper Moscow gate (1765)

9. Lower Moscow gate (1779)

10. Gunpowder magazine (1755)

11. Vasylkiv Ravelin gate (1755)

12. Gunpowder cellar (1749-1751)

13. The Church of Our Saviour at Berestovo

14. Remains of fortification rampart (1706-1720)

15. General-governor's house (1757-1759, 1780)

III New Pechersk Fortress

16. Fortification wall around the Near and Far Caves (1844-
1848)

17. Military cantonists' barracks (1835-1839, today – Academy
for Communications, 45 Moskovska Street)

18. Tower No. 4 (1833-1839, 47 Moskovska Street)

19. Tower No. 5 (1833-1846, 16 Pechersky Descent)

20. Gendarmerie regiment barracks (1844-1847, 22 Moskovska
Street)

21. Tower No. 6 (1846-1851, 8 Moskovska Street)

22. Arsenal workshops (1850-1854) /ARSENAL Works/

23. Nickolas' gate with the adjacent barracks
(1848-1850). The main entrance led through the bridge (did not
preserve) to Mariinsky Palace

24. Upper support wall (1853-1855, today – the Green Theatre,
2 Parkova Road)

25. Lower support wall (1856, Naberezhne Highway)

A. Vasylkivske Fortification

26. 'Round' tower No. 2 (1833-1844, 44 Schorsa Street)

27. Caponier (1833-1837)

28. 'Prozorovskaya' tower No. 3 (1838-1839, the Field Marshal
A. Prozorovsky is buried in the Church of Sts. Prince Volodymyr and
Alexander Nevsky)

29. Reduit tower No. 1 (1831-1837, 38 Schorsa Street)

30. Stone gorge (rear) wall (1831-1837) /Partly preserved/

31. Ramparts and ditches (1832-1839, 59 Chygorina Str. – 8 Per-
spektyvna Str.)

B. Hospital Fortification

32. Hospital (1836-1842)

33. Caponier No. 1 of polygonal front (1843-1844)

34. Caponier No. 2 of polygonal front (1843-1844)

35. Oblique caponier (1844-1846)

36. Northern half-tower (1839-1842)

37. Northern gate (1843-1844)

38. Central caponier(1843-1844)

39. Caponier No. 3 of polygonal front (1844)

C. Zvirynetske Fortification (1810-1812) /fragments preserved/

40. Vydubytsky Monastery with fortification walls

D. Lysohirsky Fort (1872-1876)

Upper Moscow gate (1765)

Northern half-tower of Hospital fortification. The view from Northern gate

One of 12 galleries of Lysohirsky fort (1872-1876)

Defensive wall near the Bell Tower at the Far Caves (1844-1848)

Nickolas' gate (1848-1850)

Arsenal building (1784-1798) in front of the Holy gate of Lavra

Ivan Kuschnyk tower (1698-1701)

wide in the bottom part, up to 7 m high. Four towers of five have been preserved: the **East tower** (or St. Onuphry tower, or the Palatna, i.e. Chamber tower), the **Southwest tower** (or the tower of Ivan Kuschnyk), the **North tower** (or the Malyarna, i.e. the Painter's tower), and the **South tower** (or **Horlogium** —it had a clock until 1818). A system of underground brick layered passages with niches was arranged along the whole perimeter at a depth of 7 metres under the wall foundation bottom. This enabled digging out passages towards saps. The whole underground complex for storing armaments, foodstuffs, and ammunition was also arranged in Upper Lavra.

Being at war with Sweden, *Peter I* made Kyiv a strategic defense base. The construction of a mighty fortress started on August 15, 1706 according to his design. The works were supervised by *Ivan Mazepa* (assisted by *Lamotte de Tampi*). After the Battle at Poltava (1709) they were carried out by European experts (*Brekling*, et al.) The semicircular fortress consisted of earth ramparts 6 to 20 metres high, nine bastions with one demi-bastion strengthened with 3 ravelins at the northern west. Dry ditches 5 to 6 metres deep and 40 metres wide were arranged in front of the ramparts. Three gates led to the fortress, two of them have been preserved till our days: the South, or **Moscow gate**, and the West, or **Vasylkiv gate**. The fortress was reached through drawbridges.

In 1712 Hetman *I. Skoropadsky's* Cossacks built a 3-kilometre-long rampart – retrenchment – that connected Pechersk and Starokyivska Fortresses. Lunettes – underground brick-layered galleries filled with gunpowder that were blown up when enemy was attacking – were arranged within the fortress' territory. The whole Pechersk – from Arsenalna underground station to the Olympiysky Sports Complex – abounds in such undergrounds.

The above-mentioned fortress was completed in 1723. Then in 1749-1751 the engineer *D. de Bosquet* built gunpowder cellars, and the **Arsenal** was added in 1784-1798 according to the design of *I. Meller*. The monumental building of Arsenal built in Classic style is 600 metres long along the perimeter. Now it is being restored for the **Mystetsky Arsenal** ('Arts Arsenal') Museum Complex.

On the eve of the 1812 Russian-French war the Kyiv Governor-General *M. Kutuzov* initiated the construction of the **Zvirynetske fortification** designed by the military engineer *Karl Oppermann* (1765-1831). Four redoubts connected it with the **Pechersk Fortress**.

Under the Emperor *Nickolas I*, the **Old Pechersk Fortress** was strengthened and transformed into the citadel of the **New Fortress**. The construction began in 1830. Having an area of 70 hectares, it became one of the biggest and the most up-to-date fortresses in Europe.

The **Vasylkivske fortification** was built on the south-western part of Pechersk highlands. It consisted of three towers linked with a fortress wall,

The view on the caponier, Olympic Stadium, the Northern half-tower (1839-1844), and the Northern gate of Hospital fortification

Oblique caponier (1843-1844)

The view on the Hospital fortification (1843-1846)

earth ramparts, and a ravelin with a caponier. **Tower No. 4** with military cantonists' barracks was built in the south-east along Navodnytsky ravine; **Tower No. 5**, over Pechersky Descent; and **Tower No. 6**, over Klovsky ravine. The Hospital fortification included the **hospital buildings** with the latest equipment for 1500 seats (established in 1755), **three caponiers** in ditches, **Kosoy** (Oblique) **caponier**, **Northern gate** with **Central caponier** and a **bridge, Northern half-tower**, 10-15-meterhigh earth ramparts, and deep ditches. The fortification was built at Cherepanova hill in 1836-1849. The multileveled defence system made the fortress unassailable. One cannot but be impressed with Kosoy caponier, an semisubterranean structure, with embrasures and loopholes for cannons and guns, located at the angle to the earth rampart. Since 1863 it was used as a prison for political convicts, primarily for the participants of the 1863-1864 Polish Uprising. Now it houses the **Pechersk Fortress Museum**.

To satisfy increased needs of New Fortress **new Arsenal** workshops were built in 1850-1854. **Nicholas' gate** *á la Gothic style* with adjacent barracks, the main entrance to New Pechersk Fortress, is located nearby. A wooden bridge with drawn-up spans led to it from **Mariinsky Palace**. The year's foodstuffs for the 20,000 garrison and armaments for 100,000 army were kept in the fortress warehouses. The water from the Dnieper was delivered to the fortress to a height of 107 m by 'cable planes', with a network of wells being arranged in case of emergency.

After rifle artillery had appeared, casemate structures lost their defensive significance, so the famous military engineer *E. I. Totleben* developed a project for a belt of 27 earth **forts** located around the fortress. But only one of them – the biggest in the world – was built in 1872 at illomened **Lysa Hora**. Its area is 1.2 sq. km.

Most fortress structures have been well preserved and represent brilliantly versatile fortification systems as well as examples of fortification architecture from the mid- 17th c. till the late 19th c. The sizes and might of Kyiv Fortress really impress. This may be the reason why the enemy never attacked it. The fame about its inaccessibility and its redoubtable view forced the enemy to pass Kyiv and allowed the city to develop rapidly.

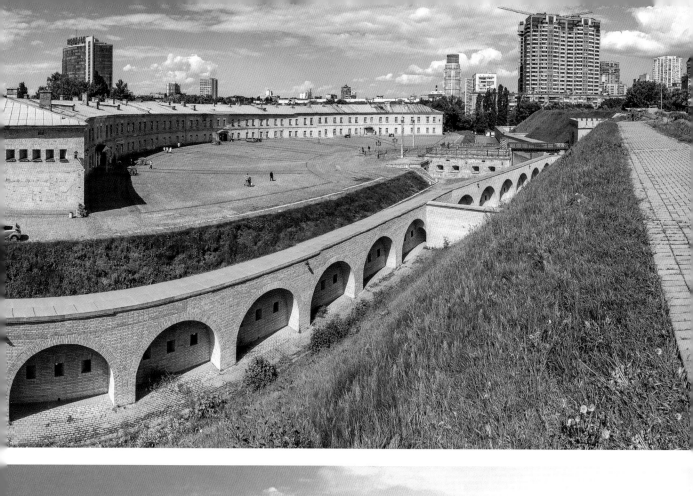

Museums and Residences

Kyiv is a city of museums. Some of them have already been mentioned above. It would be impossible to describe all of them, so we will tell you about the most notable ones. But let us mention government residences first. These are buildings in which the President of Ukraine receives official foreign delegations and foreign leaders. The most notable among them are **Mariinsky Palace** and the **'House with Chimeras'**.

The National Museum for the History of Ukraine (2 Volodymyrska Street, phone: +380 44 278 48 64, http://www.nmiu.org.ua) was founded in 1904. Its collection totals above 800,000 unique monuments of history and culture, including numerous archaeological findings, valuable painting, graphics, and sculpture, a lot of cold and fire arms, ethnography, glassware and porcelain, etc. Relics of Zaporozhian Cossacks – Cossack symbols, universals, charters, letters of hetmans and Cossack nobility are widely presented. The numismatic collection numbers more than 100,000 units. The museum is located in the building dating back to 1939 (by *I. Karakis*).

The Historical Treasures Museum (phone: +38044 280 13 96, http://www.miku.org.ua). The museum is situated at the territory of Kyiv-Pechersk Lavra at **Kovnir Building**. The highlight is the display of a golden Scythian pectoral (breast ornament) and a silver vase both dated to the 4th c. B.C. There is also an extensive collection of artefacts made of precious stones in 6th-12th cc. by Rus masters, collection of jewellery made by Russian goldsmiths in 16th-19th cc., and a unique collection of Jewish ritual silver (18th– early 20th cc.).

The exposition of the **Museum of the History of Kyiv** (2 Khreschatyk Str., phone: +38044 278 12 40) contains about 200,000 original exhibits and includes archaeological, culturological, and ethnographic collections. There are collections of icons, artefacts, personal belongings of Kyivites of different centuries and good collection of photographs. The museum has a network of branches, The House of Peter I, Heritage Museum in Pechersk, etc.

The National Art Museum of Ukraine (6 Hrushevskoho Str., phone: +38044 278 13 57, 278 74 54, http://namu.kiev.ua). The museum occupies the building decorated with lions which was built by *V. Horodetsky* according to the design of *P. Boytsov* in 1897-1899. The sculptural decoration was made by *E. Sala*. Different trends in the Ukrainian art are presented in the museum. The museum features the collection of ancient icons, the most valuable of them are 'St. George with Life' (11th c.) from St. George monastery situated not far from Sevastopol and the icon of the Mother of God 'The Protecting Veil' (the early 13th c.). A unique collection of folk paintings of the 18th-19th cc. can be found in the museum. There is also a collection of portraits of Ukrainian Hetmans and officers of Cossacks Army dating to the 18th c. There is also a collection of works of Ukrainian avant-garde painters *A. Ekster, A. Bogomazov, V. Yermilov*, and others.

The National Museum of Taras Shevchenko (12 Shevchenka Blvd., phone: +38044 234 25 23, http://www.shevchenkomuseum.com.ua). In the 19th c. this building belonged to the mayor of Kyiv *P. Demidov*, later it became a mansion of the outstanding entrepreneur and patron of arts *N. Tereschenko*. The museum's collection of more than 80,000 exhibits is composed of the poet's personal belongings, his paintings and etchings, copies and original manuscripts of his poems, rare photographs. Besides the above-mentioned house of Shevchenko at the alley named after the poet, there is another building in Kyiv where Shevchenko lived in August, 1859 (5 Vyshhorodska Str.). Nowadays the Memorial House-Museum of Taras Shevchenko is situated there. **National University** is named after the great Ukrainian poet as well and is known as Taras Shevchenko University. On the front wall of the main University building constructed in 1837-1842 one can find a memorial plaque to the poet. Opposite the main University building in a picturesque park that was also named after the poet you can find a **monument to Taras Shevchenko** that was erected in 1939.

National Art Museum
of Ukraine:

*St. George with Life.
11*[th]* (?) c. Byzantium*

*Christ in Majesty. Latter
half of 15*[th]* c. Halychyna*

*Anonymous painter.
The portrait of Hetman
Zinoviy-Bohdan
Khmelnytsky. Mid-18*[th]* c.
B. Khmelnytsky has a
mace in his hands. Mace
is an ancient weapon
used in Western Europe
and Rus state since
the 11*[th]* c. until 19*[th]* c. it
had been the attribute
of power of Polish and
Ukrainian hetmans*

*A. Ekster. Three Women
Figures. 1910*

**Taras Shevchenko
National Museum:**

*Paintings by
T. Shevchenko:
St. Alexander's Roman-
Catholic Cathedral in
Kyiv. Watercolour. 1846*

*The Church of All Saints
in Kyiv-Pechersk Lavra.
Sepia. 1846*

Kyiv Russian Art Museum:

M. Vrubel.
Girl Against Persian Carpet

K. Makovsky.
Girl In Ukrainian Dress

White Hall interiors

Mariinsky Palace. *White Hall*

House with Chimeras.
Small dining-hall

On page 126 – 127:
Historical Treasures Museum:

Quiver Plaque. Scythia. 4th B.C.

*Torah-Shield. Odesa. Ukraine.
The late 19th c.*

*Kolts (headdress pendants).
Ancient Rus. 11th – 13th cc.*

*Pyx. By craftsman S. Taranovsky.
Kyiv. 18th c.*

125

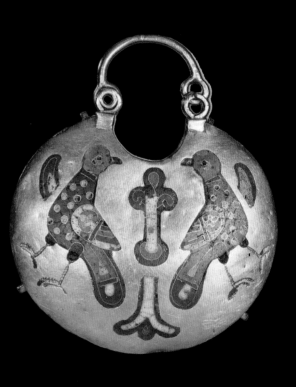

The Museum of Lesia Ukrainka (phone: +38044 287 50 46, 289 57 52). *Lesia Ukrainka* (the pen name of *Larysa Kosach*) is a well-known Ukrainian poetess. The museum is situated at 97 Saksahanskoho Street. Lesia Ukrainka stayed here between 1899 and 1910 with her mother *Olena Pchilka*. She wrote a lot of her famous poems while being here. The museum collection displays personal belongings of the poetess, manuscripts and first editions of her works. There is a **monument** to Lesia Ukrainka that was erected at the square named after this renowned Ukrainian poetess. Opposite Mariinsky Palace in the park you can find a graceful **sculpture** of Lesia Ukrainka by V. Borodai and A. Ihnaschenko. Next to it there is also a sculpture of the outstanding Ukrainian actress *Maria Zankovetska* by H. Kalchenko. She lived in Kyiv at 121 Velyka Vasylkivska Street, where a **museum** is located now.

The Museum of Theatrical, Musical and Cinema Arts of Ukraine (phone: +38044 280 18 34, http://www.tmf-museum.kiev.ua/ua/main_ie.htm). The museum is situated at the territory of Kyiv-Pechersk Lavra. The museum numbers more than 200,000 exhibits of the 18th-20th cc. and posseses archives of outstanding representatives of Ukrainian culture – *M. Kropyvnytsky, I. Karpenko-Kary, P. Saksahansky, M. Lysenko*, and many others.

Bohdan and Varvara Khanenko Museum of Art (15-17 Tereschenkivska Str., phone: +38044 235 32 90, http://www.khanenkomuseum.kiev.ua). The museum was founded in 1919 on the basis of the private collection of Kyiv archeologist *Bohdan Khanenko*. The Green Cabinet features the collection of Medieval Art, the Golden Cabinet contains objects of Rococo epoch and in the Red Cabinet you can find paintings of Renaissance period. There are 17,000 exhibits in the museum funds. Among the exhibits are the paintings of *J. Bellini, F. Hals, J. L. David, J. Reynolds, P. P. Rubens, F. de Zurbaran*, masterpiece 'Infanta Margarita' by *D. Velazquez*, and unique Byzantine icons of the 6th-7th cc. painted in wax paints. Interesting exhibits are presented at the Oriental Art section: piece of Coptic fabric with the picture of horseman (5th-6th cc.), ritual Chinese bell (1st c. B.C.), excellent Chinese paintings on the scrolls (15th-20th cc.), Japanese paintings, and a rare collection of the details of sword handles (15th-19th cc.).

The Kyiv Museum of Russian Art (9 Tereschenkivska Str., phone: +38044 234 62 18, http://www.kmrm.com.ua). The museum is situated in the former mansion of *F. Tereschenko* built in 1882-1884. The exposition of the museum has an outstanding collection of Russian icons dated to 12th-18th cc., including a precious icon 'Boris and Gleb', and masterpieces by *I. Repin, M. Vrubel, N. Rerikh, I. Aivazovsky, B. Kustodiev, N. Ge, I. Shishkin*, and many others.

The State Museum of Ukrainian Folk Decorative Art (phone: +38044 280 36 93, http://www.mundm.kiev.ua). The museum was opened in metropolitan's house dated to the 18th c. and in Annunciation metropolitan's church dated to 1905 at the territory of Kyiv-Pechersk Lavra. It contains the richest collection of Ukrainian folk art of the 15th-20th cc. including embroidery, wood carving, ceramics, art glass, china, faience, carpets, pysankas (painted eggs). Special expositions cover works of painters *Kateryna Bilokur* and *Maria Prymachenko*.

The Ukrainian Museum of Book and Book Printing (phone: +38044 280 79 76) is located in the premises of the former Lavra printing house. The collection, totalling 52,000 items, presents the history of the book from Kyivan Rus times till our days. The collection includes unique samples of the 16th-18th cc. books published in Kyiv-Pechersk, Lviv, Ostrih, Univ, Pochaiv, Chernihiv, and Moscow printing houses; the first editions of Ukrainian writers and poets.

The Miniatures Museum of Mykola Siadrysty (at the territory of Kyiv-Pechersk Lavra, building No. 5, phone: +38044 280 81 37). A unique collection of Ukrainian craftsman *M. Siadrysty* is presented at the exposition. The works displayed here will hit your imagination. He not only managed to shoe a flea, you will also be able to see a beautiful 0.05 mm rose that was put inside a well-polished human hair or a model of frigate called 'Scarlet Sails' that is 5 mm long. It consists of 337 parts, and rigging is 400 times thinner than a human hair. All these works are hand-made by *M. Siadrysty*.

The Museum of Ukrainian Hetmans. The museum is situated at 16B Spasska Street (phone: +38044 462 52 90, http://www.getman-museum.kiev.ua). Separate halls of the museum cover the lives of Hetman *Ivan Mazepa* and Hetman *Pavlo Skoropadsky*.

The Museum 'Kyrylivska Church' (St. Cyril's Church). 12 Telihy Str., phone: +38044 468 11 26. The church was built in 1146 and was used as a family burial vault of Princes *Olgovychi* of Chernihiv. Prince *Svyatoslav Vsevolodovych*, one of the heroes of the chronicle 'The Lay of the Host of Igor', was buried in this church in 1194. Here you can see 800 sq. m of 12th century frescos and majestic wall paintings by *M. Vrubel* including a famous 'The Mother of God with a Baby'.

State Aviation Museum (1 Medova Str., phone: +38044 461-64-85, http://www.avia-museum.org.ua). The display includes sixty exhibits. Among them you can find the following models of airplanes: IL, MIG, SU, AN, TU, rare specimens B-6, B-12, as well as helicopter MI-26. Visitors have an opportunity not only to see and touch the airplanes that reflect the history of Ukrainian aviation but also get into the cockpit.

The Chemist's Shop Museum at Podil in the chemist's building dated to 1818-1820 can be found at 7 Prytysko-Mykilska Street (phone: +38044 425 24 37). The first chemist's shop in Kyiv was opened in 1728 in the building that used to stand at this site. The laboratory of chemist, the cabinet of a healer, and a monk's cell were restored and opened for tourists.

Water-information center 'The Museum of Water' is situated in the 19th-century water tower near Yevropeyska Square (phone: +38044 279 53 33, http://www.aqua-kiev.info). The exposition tells about the role of the water in our life, the system of operating the centralized water supply and water drainage, and the process of water treatment. Here you will see a functioning model of artesian well; a gigantic lavatory pan; a fairy-tale grotto with a waterfall, rain, thunder, and lightning, etc.

Cultural life in Kyiv

Gallery space Cultprostir Hub at the History of Kyiv museum. The exhibition 'Museum Collection' by Anatoliy Kryvolap

Art space 'ArtPrichal'. Photo exhibition by Yuriy Kosin (2015)

GogolFEST-2012. Platforma Art Factory

The biggest Kyiv cultural, arts and museum complex is **MYSTETSKYI ARSENAL** (Art Arsenal) located within the territory of Old Pechersk Fortress Arsenal and occupying the area of 50,000 sq m/ 59,800 sq yd. Its halls are used to demonstrate performances and modern art exhibitions of the best Ukrainian and foreign artists, museum collections, retrospectives and antique saloons. Many of them are initiated and created by Ms *Natalia Zabolotna*, Director General. In 2012, the center hosted the First Kyiv International Contemporary Art Biennale ARSENALE 2012. The prominent British art gallery curator *David Elliott* collected 250 emblematic works of contemporary artists from 30 countries of the world. Impressive installations were demonstrated within the exposition area of 24 thou sq m/ 28.7 thou sq yd, art groups and theater companies performed. Parallel to the main program, special cultural projects were placed at other 35 venues of the city.

Another major international center of the 21ˢᵗ c. contemporary arts is housed at **PinchukArtCentre.** This is an open experimental platform for artists, arts and the society, uniting national identification and international challenges. Noticeable cultural projects take

place at municipal gallery 'Lavra' (9 Lavrskyi Lane), in museums History of Kyiv (space Cultprostir Hub, 7 Bohdana Khmelnitskoho Str.), NAMU and in 'Sofia of Kyiv', DUKAT gallery (8b Reitarskaya Str.), M17 gallery (102-104 Antonovycha Str.), Museum of Modern Arts of Ukraine (41 Frunze Str.), in ArtHall D12 private museum (12 Desyatinna Str.). The latter represents a big collection of icons created at 14th c. – 20th c., Russian and Western-European art.

Opening of the monument to K. Malevich by Spanish sculptor Carlos Garcia Lajoz in National Academy of Fine Art and Architecture

Mural 'Flipping Gymnast Anna Rizatdinova' (2016, 12 Streletskaya Str., art. Fintan Megi)

In recent years ART-spaces are becoming more popular: IZONE (8 Naberezhno-Lugovaya Str.); ArtPrichal (berth No.2), PLATFORMA art-factory (1a Belomorskaya Str.), Malaya Opera (5 Degtyarevskaya Str.); KPI Tower (Main building), TYKVA (72 Glubochitskaya Str.), ATMASFERA 360 (Planetarium), Master Klass House (16a Lavrska Str.).

Street art is increasingly popular in Kyiv. In place of the mosaic panel of the Soviet period of 1960-70-ies murals came into the urban streetscape. They are made not only by talented Ukrainian authors, but also by famous artists from Spain, Australia, Brazil, France, England, Portugal and Poland.

Theater director and playwright *Vladislav Troitskyi* has established the DAKH (Roof) Center for Modern Arts and the annual GogolFEST festival. The festival merges music, dancing, experimental theater, painting, design, cinema and audiovisual arts within the single interactive space and is enormously popular among the youth.

Mural 'Life without science – death' (2013, façade 2 of Kyiv Mohyla Academy building, art. J. Mallan (Seth), V. Manzhos (Waone))

Chocolate House. Chocolate seasons-2016. Fashion show of designer Polina Veller within 'Women's Art Project'

Malanka at Mystetskyi Arsenal

The First Kyiv International Biennial of Contemporary Art ARSENALE 2012. At Mystetskyi Arsenal – visitors among the installation of the Japanese sculptor Shigeo Toya 'Wood IX'

ART-spaces ATMASFERA 360

Since 2004, the multi-genre Printemps Francais (**French Spring**) Festival supported by the French Embassy to Ukraine and Alliance Francaise (French Institute in Kyiv) has been held. In the course of **Ivan Kupala Folk Feast** (corresponds to the John the Baptist Day; early June) the Singing Field hosts the International Ethnic Festival KRAYINA MRIY (Dreamland) founded by popular Ukrainian musician *Oleh Skrypka*. It combines fair festivities with performances of ethnic groups coming from various countries, folk dances, Cossack entertainments, and exhibition of folk craftsmen goods. During the festival all visitors may taste unique ethnic cuisine dishes, and visit folk craft master classes.

The **Kiev Fire Fest** – an international fire festival started in 2007 – has become widely known. The audience may enjoy a vivid show of the best fire maestros and theaters from different countries. The international festival of arts 'Anne de Kiev Fest' is held since 2015. It dedicated to Princess *Anne de Kiev* and her role in world history. The annual theater Wandering Stars festival is dedicated to the creative activities of the Jewish culture classic *Sholem Aleichem*, and

Art-project 'Botany' at the Municipal Gallery 'Lavra'

3-D light-show 'Anuki in search of spring' on the façade of the Ukrainian House. The opening of 'French Spring-2016'

Opening of 'NSC Olimpiyskiy' (2011). Shakira's performance

On page 134: Fireworks above Kyiv

the International Competition for Young Pianists in Memory of *Vladimir Horowitz* is held in Kyiv in honour of an outstanding Kyiv piano player *Vladimir Horowitz*.

Table of Contents

Concept, text preparation, selection of photographs – **Sergei Udovik**
Adviser –**Svetlana Guzenko, Ph. D.**
Translation – **Larissa Udovik** (New York, USA), **Kateryna Lakhovskaya** (Kyiv, Ukraine), **Edit Ganish** (Kyiv, Ukraine), **Daryna Trotsan** (Kyiv, Ukraine). Thanks for editing **Ihor Ciszkewycz**

PHOTOS. Legend: T-top, TR-top right, TL-top left, TC-top center, B-bottom, BR-bottom right, BL-bottom left

Sergei Udovik: *front* cover, *pages 3-12, 13 (TR, BR), 14, 15B, 16-18, 19T, 20B, 21-33, 35-39, 40BR, 41, 42BR, 43BR, 44-77, 78B, 79-81, 84-91, 92T. 92BL, 93-98, 99-121, 125B, 128-133;*
Eugeny Savakov: *back* cover, *pages 19B, 34, 82-83, 99;*
Oleh Romanovskyi: *page 13TL;*
The National Art Museum of Ukraine: *pages 15T, 122;*
The National Taras Shevchenko Museum: *pages 20T, 123;*
Sergei Savchenko: *pages 78T, 134;*
Oleh Karataev: *page 92BR*
O. Fedorenko: *page 124TL;*

Mikhail Andreyev: *pages 124B, 126-127;*
International Book, Moscow: *page 124TR;*
V. Nosikov, Fuji-Sport *company: page 125T;*
UNIAN: *Valeriy Solovyov - page 38T; Volodymyr Gontar - page 38BL, 43TC; Sergiy Svetlitsky - page 43TR; UNIAN - p. 43BL*
From Wikipedia: *page 42BΛ - User File Upload Bot (Magnus Manske); page 42BR- Participant Shakko; page 42C - Participant Ras67; Photo of Milla Jovich (page 43BL) - from site http://www.popcornnews.ru/tag/9551*

The Publishing Company expresses its gratitude to *Yury Solominsky* for the permition to use the image of the Coat of Arms of Kyiv City developed by him.

The Publishing Company would like to express great thanks to the Administration of the President of Ukraine and The State Department for Affairs of Ukraine for the assistance in preparing the book.

The Publishing Company would like to express the gratitude for the assistance in preparing the photo album to the Kyiv City Council, the Ministry for Culture and Tourism of Ukraine, the Main Department for the Culture and Arts and the Main Department for Cultural Heritage Protection of the Kyiv City Government Administration, the Bohdan and Varvara Khanenko Museum of Art, Kyiv National Museum of Russian Art, the National Art Museum of Ukraine, the National Taras Shevchenko Museum, the National Natural Science Museum, the One Street Museum, the House-Museum of Mykola Lysenko, Taras Schevchenko National Opera of Ukraine, the *Suziria* Dramatic Art Studio, the administration of the Kyiv Pechersk National Historical and Cultural Reserve.

S. Udovik. Kyiv. Photo book. – eighth edition – Kyiv: Vakler Publishing Company, 2016. – 136 p. – У 31 ('The Cities of Ukraine' series).

ISBN 978-966-543-086-7 (series)
ISBN 978-966-543-106-0

The richly illustrated book deals with eventful history of Kyiv. The sights of the city are presented in the form of walks through Kyiv. Certain chapters cover Kyiv Pechersk Lavra, Podil, Khreschatyk, present-day Kyiv, parks, monasteries, Kyiv Art Nouveau, Kyiv fortresses (with the scheme of Pechersk Fortress), sport and famous Kyivans, cultural life of Kyiv. The book contains 290 colour photographs.

УДК 908 (477-25) (084.12)=161

Sergei Udovik
KYIV
Photo book

Cover design *Valery Chutur*
CRPU and image editing *Vladislav Udovik*
Outline map on endpaper *Olesya Silakova, Vladislav Udovik*
Outline map of Kyiv Fortress (pp. 112-113) *Sergey Udovik* and *Bohdan Petrov*

Printed and bound in Kyiv (Ukraine)

Підписано до друку 12.06.2016. Формат 84х108/16, папір крейдований 130 г/м². Друк офсетний. Видавництво "Ваклер" у формі товариства з обмеженою відповідальністю, свідоцтво про внесення до державного реєстру суб'єкта видавничої справи ДК №3890 від 07.10.2010, Київ, вул. Рибальська 13. Тел. +38-067-220-8882, e-mail: vakler@ukr.net. Адреса для листування: 04070, Київ-70, а/с 67. Видавництво "Ваклер".

З питань дрібно-оптової торгівлі звертатися за тел.: (044) 496-04-70 (71). Книги видавництва можна придбати в інтернет-книгарні www.odissey.kiev.ua

Видавництво намагалося навести уточнені дані станом на 31.03.2016 щодо назв вулиць та різних установ, які згадані у фотокнизі. За можливі розбіжності Видавництво попередньо перепрошує.

Друк: Віддруковано у ТОВ "ПК Типографія від А до Я"
02660, м. Київ, вул. Колекторна, 38/40, тел. (044) 563 1804
Свідоцтво про державну реєстрацію ДК №405 від 06.04.01

Зам. № 1544